111 Ways To Justify Your Commission

Value-Adding Strategies for Real Estate Agents and Brokers

Michael Soon Lee

KAPLAN PUBLISHING

New York

This publication is designed to provide accurate and authoritative information in regard to the subject matter covered. It is sold with the understanding that the publisher is not engaged in rendering legal, accounting, or other professional service. If legal advice or other expert assistance is required, the services of a competent professional should be sought.

Editorial Director: Jennifer Farthing
Acquisitions Editor: Michael Sprague
Development Editor: Mary Good
Production Editor: Fred Urfer
Production Artist: Janet Schroeder

Published by Kaplan Publishing,
a Division of Kaplan, Inc.

Printed in the United States of America

August 2007

07 08 09 10 9 8 7 6 5 4 3 2 1

ISBN: 978-1-4277-5470-7

DEDICATION

To my wife, Miriam, and our sons, Ryan and Christopher, who sacrificed so much to help make this book a reality. This book is also dedicated to the hundreds of real estate professionals who lent ideas and suggestions to make sure it had unique value for the readers.

C o n t e n t s

I believe that the current demand for lower real estate commissions is the result of two things: increased competition in our industry, and decreased value. As markets improve, more people get into the business. The newer agents don't know how to compete on value so they compete on price. It seems their belief is, "Because someone asks me to cut my fee I have to cut my fee." It's the easiest answer for them but ultimately the most painful. They end up working for less, then resent themselves for having reduced their commission. They also have less money available to market the property and just end up working harder for less money.

When I ask experienced agents why they cut their fee they usually say, "It's to get more listings and maintain market share." My answer is, "Market share is for kids—profit is for adults." The way to increase profit is through maintaining your margins, not just market share. If you give good service and good value you can gain both. Given the choice of losing the listing or losing money, I'd rather lose the listing.

There is a belief among agents that by making a bit less on each transaction they'll make it up in volume. If they would actually do the math they'd learn that reducing the commission by 1 percent requires about a 20 percent increase in units to break even.

The single best solution to maintaining a reasonable number of closed units and getting paid well for them is to deliver value. What I like about Michael Lee's book is that it offers specific ways to deliver value and to explain that value to clients.

I suggest that real estate agents ask the owners this question: "At the time you purchased your present car, were there less expensive options available? Why did you knowingly pay more for this one?"

Their answers will establish their belief that it is worth paying more for additional value.

Value is crucial today for agent survival and success. For example, in my video "Selecting Your Real Estate Agent," I show owners the eight essential steps that must occur in order for a home to be sold, and how to recognize the value an agent delivers in each of those steps.

In my seminars I can show agents how to create value but it's up to them to take action to provide that value. I believe that a book that has 111 ways to do this is a great written tool to help people go forth and sell their value to their clients.

David S. Knox, CRS
National Real Estate Trainer
Minneapolis, Minnesota

Today, more clients than ever are questioning the value of real estate services and asking agents to reduce their commissions. In fact, the average commission rate dropped 16 percent in the last 14 years. (This is according to the latest research from industry analyst REAL Trends.)

Unfortunately, it is expected that there will continue to be downward pressure on commissions because technology has made it possible for clients to conduct many real estate activities for themselves online. For example, buyers can look for the home of their dreams over the Internet right from their own home, surfing the Web while still in their pajamas. Sellers can use the same technology to advertise their property worldwide over the Internet, bypassing the formerly exclusive REALTOR® Multiple Listing Service. What everyone seems to forget is that technology is only a tool; real estate is still very much a people business. In the end, successful transactions are still built on trust and the ability of the realtor to solve the clients' problems and help meet their needs.

Another challenge to commissions is the growing prevalence of discount brokers, who really emerged during the most recent real estate boom from around 1995 to 2006. They constantly implied that the public was being overcharged as home prices escalated. They constantly pointed out that they offered lower fees, which suggested that the only difference between brokers is the price, not a difference in value.

The majority of Americans now believe that we real estate professionals do little to earn our commissions. Apparently, we also make way too much money! Whose fault is it that people labor under these myths? Those of us in the real estate profession know this is far from the truth, but it is now our responsibility to prove our worth. It's not a given anymore. If we don't justify the reasons for our commissions, they will continue to drop simply because clients will not appreciate how much we do to earn them. So it is up to us to prove our value.

Compared to selling a service like real estate brokerage, selling a product like a house is relatively easy because you can simply show it to the customer. He can then see it, touch it, feel it, and make sure it works as promised. Selling service is much more difficult since you don't have the opportunity to offer a test-drive or to show people a physical object they can pick up. To sell a service you must sell value. You are essentially saying, "Pay for my time, my experience, and my knowledge and I will give you a greater return than what you will pay." To customers everywhere, value is linked to one thing: their needs. What they value the most is getting their needs met.

Even though people are different, there are certain basic needs that everyone is trying to fill, and they're not a great mystery. In this book, you will learn what these needs are, including the ones not every agent is familiar with. In addition, you will learn how to communicate with your individual client and discern what her unique needs are in a given transaction so you can address them one by one. Clients are happy when they feel listened to, when they can walk away from an interaction knowing that everything they said was perceived as important and was addressed.

This book will provide concise and practical tips about how you can meet the individual needs of your clients, so they will not only pay you what you're worth but also enthusiastically pass your name on to their friends, families, and neighbors. You will learn how to sell the value of your services to them, and how to be unique, special, and valuable so you can charge a fair price for what you provide.

ESTABLISH VALUE

I) ESTABLISH YOUR VALUE FROM THE VERY FIRST CONTACT

Every real estate professional knows he or she works hard and provides value to his or her client. Buyers pay less for a home because of our negotiating skills and are protected through disclosures and inspections. Sellers get the highest net proceeds from their houses because of the same bargaining abilities and reduced liability through disclosures and inspections. Yet, some brokers discount our value by implying that all we do is paperwork and, as a result, that consumers are being overcharged.

What is value? Simply put, value is the benefit something provides minus what it costs. You can see from this formula that there are only two ways to increase value: You can either increase the benefits provided or decrease what it costs. The choice is up to you. However, I believe that it is far more beneficial to you to do the former, and this book will show you how to identify your value and sell it to clients.

There are real estate companies that devalue the services that full-service real estate professionals provide. By offering *discount* or *limited* service they imply that the only difference between one company and another is price. You might want to remind clients that the dictionary defines the word *discount* as "a reduction made from the gross amount or value of something" and that *limited* is defined as "lacking breadth and originality." In other words, yes it costs less, but to reduce the price, the broker has to reduce value. Is this really what your client wants for one of the most important transactions of her life?

Have a frank discussion with potential clients about the dissimilarities between a full-service and a discount broker. Explain to them that there are many more differences between the two models than merely price, including services provided and liability reduction. If they still don't get it, you can also ask them why a stripped-down car costs less than a fully loaded one. This analogy should help anyone understand what's really at stake.

Since value is created in the minds of our clients, we must first find out what they value. Throughout this book you will learn ways to determine this by asking probing questions and listening. One of the biggest mistakes you can make is to assume you know what someone wants. In general, people might have a lot in common, especially when they are buying or selling a house, but there are so many ways that they are unique. If you want to know what differentiates one person from another, you have to be interested enough to ask. However, having said that, there are certain needs that are universal; let's look at the following basic expectations that most people have of their real estate agents:

Sellers

- Maximizing sales price
- Saving them time
- Minimizing inconvenience
- Receiving regular progress reports from their agent

- Saving money when preparing the house for sale
- Developing creative marketing strategies
- Delivering a competent listing presentation
- Giving them the confidence that their agent can do the job
- Providing a reasonable listing period
- Reducing their liability
- Educating them about the selling process

Buyers

- Saving them money by minimizing their purchase price
- Saving time in finding an appropriate property
- Offering them a wide variety of properties in their price range
- Showing them properties in an efficient way
- Writing a purchase agreement that accurately reflects their desires
- Negotiating a superior deal
- Informing them about inspections that are available
- Educating them about the buying process
- Providing regular progress reports

By showing how you meet these needs and more, you begin to establish value in the minds of your clients.

2) COMPETE ON VALUE, NOT ON PRICE

What specialized skill or training does it take to compete on price? Absolutely none! All you have to do is offer the lowest price and all those people who don't want to open their wallets will flock to you like flies to the compost pail.

There are a couple of problems, however, with competing on price. The first is that you cannot have the lowest price all the time. Somebody can undercut you in a heartbeat. You might have read about or even remember the gas price wars of the 1960s, when there were gas stations on just about every corner. Whenever one station owner would lower his price, the others would quickly follow suit. Instead of gaining market share, all this clever dealer did was begin to eliminate his and everyone else's profit margin.

The second problem with competing on price is that people do not necessarily buy the cheapest product on the market. Studies show that while 15 percent of shoppers are primarily motivated by price, the majority (80 percent) consider other factors such as quality, service, reliability, and reputation to be more important. Plus, 5 percent of shoppers are actually motivated by a higher price because it implies greater quality and a real caché.

All you have to do is ask prospects to consider choices in other areas of their lives. They could buy the cheapest car, the most basic computer, cut-rate health care, a bottom-of-the-barrel home entertainment system, and bargain basement clothes from The Salvation Army. Do they? Some do—and that's why manufacturers make entry-level products—but are these the kind of clients you want?

Explain to your clients that providing quality service takes time, experience, and training. These do not come cheap and people who appreciate quality are willing to pay for it. In fact, research by Alcatel-Lucent has shown that customers who perceive high quality in a product will be prepared to pay a premium price. Some people always buy the most expensive products assuming they will be of the highest quality.

3) MAKE A LIST OF ACTIVITIES YOU DO TO EARN YOUR COMMISSION

One of the most effective ways to visibly demonstrate your value to clients is to write out a list of the activities you engage in to earn your commission. When I started in real estate, I made a list of over 100 things I had to do to sell a house. Just a few of these things were the following:

- Obtain a preliminary title report
- Develop a targeted marketing plan
- Show potential buyers the property
- Hold the property open
- Place advertising in appropriate media
- Negotiate on behalf of the seller

I had no idea how powerful a list like this could be until one day a seller asked me to lower my commission because "You agents don't do that much." I then whipped out my well-prepared list and said, "I don't know about other agents, but I earn my money. These are just some of things I do for my commission. If you want me to lower it, pick a few of the tasks you would be willing to do instead of me because each one takes time." The seller's eyes usually glaze over at the pages of detail required to close a deal and he always says, "You're the agent, I expect you to do these things for me." Upon which my response was, "That's fine. I will do everything I believe it will take to sell your house for the highest price, but then you have to pay me what I'm worth. If you want to pay less, I'll see if I can find you an agent who will do less and maybe they can save you some money."

In over 30 years, I've never met a seller who wanted to do any of the things on that list. In fact, after they see my list, and after I explain how little real estate agents really earn, they usually say, "You guys are overworked and underpaid!" The moment you hear this, you'll know you've justified your commission.

I've also developed a list of over one hundred things I do to earn my money when working with buyers. It's even longer than the sellers' list because helping a client buy a home takes more time and work. My list includes such activities as the following:

- Locate appropriate properties that meet the buyer's wants and needs
- Educate the buyer about financing options
- Arrange for inspections as requested by the buyer

- Write a purchase offer that reflects the buyer's needs
- Negotiate the purchase on behalf of the buyer
- Open escrow

The list shows buyers just how hard I work to earn my money, which also demonstrates why they should show loyalty to me by signing a Buyer-Broker Agreement.

I've also developed similar lists for *for-sale-by-owners* (FSBOs) (100 things agents can do that sellers can't) and for *expired listings* (100 ways to get your house sold faster and at a higher price). You may want to consider coming up with similar lists if you market to FSBOs and expired listings.

4) EXPLAIN HOW THE COMMISSION IS SPLIT

One of the biggest reasons the American public doesn't appreciate our value is that they think we all make about six percent of the sales price of any property. We must educate our clients about where that money goes.

First, the commission is usually split between the listing broker and selling broker.

Then, the public is unaware that our broker charges us a third to a half of the three percent portion of the brokerage commission to cover his or her expenses, such as the following:

- Rent
- Utilities
- Computers

- Receptionist
- Training
- Manager
- Insurance
- Internet connection
- Website
- Advertising

Then, of course, agents have business expenses that can be up to 50 percent of their income which the average client, who is not self-employed, is totally unaware of, such as the following:

- Errors and omissions insurance
- National Association of REALTORS® (NAR) dues
- Local board dues
- Multiple Listing Service (MLS) fees
- Auto lease fee
- Auto insurance
- Gasoline
- Computer
- Internet connection
- Training
- Advertising
- Much more

This one percent gain is then reduced by income tax that we pay at the highest rate in the United States:

35.0% federal income tax
15.3% federal self-employment tax
10.0% state income tax (depending on which state you reside in)
60.3% total tax on the last dollar of income earned

5) EXPLAIN HOW MUCH YOU MAKE

After talking to thousands of home buyers and sellers across the country, it has become painfully clear to me that they believe we make an ungodly amount of money and that we don't do anything to earn it. They see a few of us driving Bentleys and living in Beverly Hills, and they extrapolate, incorrectly, that all real estate agents are a bunch of fat cats, that we all fit the same bill. The public thinks we sell a house every once in a while and then coast on the profits until we have to lift a finger to sell another one. In reality, according to statistics, the average agent with two years of experience or less earned $12,850 in 2005 (Pugals, 2005). And that is before taxes and expenses. For that income, you could buy a hubcap for a Bentley—and then you couldn't afford to fill it with gas.

Forget about reality. Here's what the average home buyer or seller thinks agents in his or her area earn per year (substitute your average home sales price in your area):

Average		Your Area	
$ 350,000	Average home sales price	$	
× .06	Commission		× .06
$ 21,000	Commission per house sold	$	

$ 21,000 Commission per house sold	$	
× 4 Homes they think we sell per month		× 4
$ 84,000 Income they think we get per month	$	

$ 84,000 Income they think we get per month	$	
× 12 Months in a year		× 12
$1,008,000 Income they think we get per year	$	

It's easy to see why the general public has a negative image of real estate professionals—they think we make an obscene amount of money for doing virtually nothing!

So, how much do we really make? Members of the public and even many agents don't have a clue as to what we really make. While most people think we make six percent on the sale or purchase of any property, here's the real story:

Average		Your Area
$ 350,000 Average home sales price	$	
× .06 Commission		× .06
$ 21,000 Commission per house sold	$	

$ 21,000 Commission per house sold	$	
× .50 Commission to other broker		× .50
$ 10,500 Commission to our broker	$	

$ 10,500 Commission to our broker	$	
× .67 Commission to agent		× .67
$ 7,035 Commission to agent	$	

$	7,035 Commission to agent	
	× .50 Agent expenses	× .50
$	3,518 Net income to agent	
$	3,518 Net income before tax	
	× .603 Income tax bracket	× .603
$	2,121 Income tax	
$	3,518 Net income before tax	
	− 2,121 Income tax	− 2,121
$	1,397 Net income after tax	

This is the money that we have left to feed our families, put a roof over our heads, and put our kids through school. It's not as much as people think, is it?

We must educate them about approximately how much we make. I know talking about earnings rubs some agents the wrong way, since this is a relatively taboo subject in many quarters. However, the public already assumes you make piles of money, so you might as well explain to them about commission splits and expenses, which people who work for a straight salary may not be familiar with.

EDUCATE CLIENTS ABOUT WHO REALLY PAYS THE COMMISSION

Most homeowners and many agents in the United States believe that sellers pay the real estate commission because checks to the listing broker and the selling broker are usually paid from the seller's proceeds at close of escrow. This is one of the biggest myths in real estate.

Since the beginning of organized real estate, the buyer has always paid the sales commission. This is because every seller has a net amount they must receive from the sale of their property—otherwise they will not sell. So to be sure they receive this net amount, they will add to it all the costs of sale, such as the real estate commissions, escrow fee, title fee, attorney fee (if any), transfer tax (as applicable), inspections (as appropriate), repair costs (as necessary), and any other costs they may incur.

In essence, sellers artificially raise the price of their properties to cover all the costs of sale, including our commissions. So, you can see that the buyer actually pays the commissions and closing costs through a slightly higher purchase price. Frankly, they write it off their taxes and it hardly makes any difference in the buyer's monthly mortgage payments anyway.

Here's how it works:

Amount seller wants to net	+ $
Add escrow fees	+ $
Add title fees	+ $
Add attorney fees (if any)	+ $
Add repair costs (if any)	+ $
Add other costs	+ $
Add commissions	+ $
SALES PRICE OF PROPERTY	**SALES PRICE OF PROPERTY**

If sellers truly understood that buyers pay our commission, they would actually want to raise it—because a higher fee encourages more agents to bring their buyers to look at property. This increased competition often results in a higher sales price.

7) BE PREPARED TO ANSWER COMMISSION OBJECTIONS

Since, as noted above, sellers and buyers believe we make an incredible amount of money, real estate professionals must be ready to answer common objections such as the following:

Seller objection: "Your commission is too high."
Answer 1: "Perhaps I haven't explained my value clearly. Let me show you a list of what I do to earn my money." Bring out your list of what you do to earn your fee, which should clarify the benefits to them. Essentially, it breaks everything down to the bottom line.
Answer 2: "A lot of people think we make an awful lot of money. Let me show you how much I really make on the sale of a property." Show them a pie chart or graph of how little of the total commission goes to you. This will clearly and visually make the point that you are being fair and they aren't being ripped off.

Buyer objection: "Why should I sign a Buyer-Broker Agreement with you?"
Answer: "There are a number of benefits to you in signing this agreement. For one, it allows me to show you all the properties on the market in the price range and area you want to buy. Without this agreement most agents won't do this. Another benefit to you is that I can look for properties that are not yet on the market. Without this agreement there would be no motivation for me or anyone else to do this."

Seller objection: "Other agents will list my home for a lower commission."
Answer: "Selling a house is a very complex job requiring knowledge of contracts, financing, marketing, negotiation, and more. I would hope that you would make your decision based on who can do the best job, because ultimately, a knowledgeable realtor will get you the best price and the best possible terms."

Buyer objection: "Other agents haven't asked me to sign a Buyer-Broker Agreement."

Answer: "That's because most agents aren't familiar with how this agreement benefits the buyer. Did you know that without a Buyer-Broker Agreement they won't show you all the property on the market in the price range and in the area you want to buy? I don't want to hide properties from you just because I might not get paid for showing them. I want to be able to show you everything and this agreement enables me to do that."

Seller objection: "Do you have a discounted commission?"

Answer: "The commission I charge is a discount for this reason: According to the National Association of REALTORS® statistics, if you were to try to sell your own house, you would end up with about a 16 percent lower price than if I sold it for you (NAR, 2006). If I charge you 6 percent, you're still ahead by 10 percent. So you're getting a 10 percent discount right out of the gate."

Buyer objection: "I would like to be able to work with several agents and not be exclusive with any one. I believe that gives me the best chance of finding the home of my dreams."

Answer: "I know that seems to make sense. However, smart agents will realize very quickly that you are using several of us. When that happens, they just won't put very much effort in at all. Why not trust one agent to work hard for you? That person will reward you by going the extra mile to find the home you really want. Would you like me to explain the benefits to you of signing a Buyer-Broker Agreement with me?"

Keep a list of actual commission objections you are faced with and ask experienced agents in your office or area how they would answer them. Memorize the answers and be prepared to recite them any time a client hits you with them.

8) MAKE YOUR VALUE VISIBLE TO SELLERS

Most house sellers believe that an agent does literally nothing to sell their house other than putting a sign on the lawn and an ad in the paper. To counteract this myth, develop a Sellers' Guide that educates clients on what you specifically have to offer and helps them understand the process of selling a house.

First-time sellers have no idea how to go from an initial sit-down to receiving a check for the sale of their property. This is why you must educate your sellers about the process and your part in it. The guide that I give each seller explains the process and lists over 120 things we do to earn our money.

Consider including sample contracts such as the listing agreement, purchase agreement, disclosures, and anything else that is pertinent. Not only does it show the complexity of real estate transactions, but the sheer volume implies that you provide value. Be sure that any contract you include has the word SAMPLE clearly marked across it to keep sellers from trying to use it and giving you liability.

The guide should also include appropriate and convincing articles about how to choose a real estate agent. Also, you can explain to the client, "I might be the only one sitting here, but don't be fooled. There's a whole team of people who are working to complete this complex transaction. There are lots of little helpers who are going to make this happen, like escrow and title officers, inspectors, attorneys, repair people, and many others. And I will be working closely with every one of them." Show the client the steps in the transaction, from marketing to inspections, showings, negotiations, and closing. If this leaves them reeling, all the better for you.

9) MAKE YOUR VALUE VISIBLE TO BUYERS

Besides giving buyers the same list of what you do to earn your money, consider putting together a Buyers' Guide, which explains all the aspects of buying a home. First-time buyers, as well as those who have been through this process before, need to know how to go from sitting across from you at the initial meeting to being handed the keys to their new home. They also need to be reminded of the advantages and disadvantages of home ownership including income tax deductions, potential appreciation, equity buildup, and more.

Don't forget to cover the drawbacks to home ownership as well. They can't move on short notice, they're now responsible for the cost of home repair and maintenance, and more. However, you can always make the case that, taken as a whole, the benefits to owning one's own home are overwhelmingly higher than renting and letting the landlord build all the equity.

Your Buyers' Guide should also explain the benefits of using a real estate professional.

Make sure you include articles warning about the dangers of trying to buy a house without an agent.

Do not make light of all the work involved in the purchase of a home. Again, you need to inform people that this is a complex transaction involving the coordination of many people including the seller, lender, inspectors, repair people, an escrow company, a title company, and possibly an attorney, as well as others.

10) PROVIDE SPECIALIZED/CUSTOMIZED SERVICE TO EXPIRED LISTINGS

Selling a house that has previously been on the market is much more difficult than selling a brand new listing. Be sure that the owner is clear on this fact and that you are compensated appropriately for all of the extra time and work that will be required to get it sold.

When working with expired listings, besides giving sellers a list of what you do to earn your money, consider putting together an Expired Listing Guide, which explains all the aspects of marketing a property where the listing has expired. It takes special tools and talent because a property that has been on the market for 90 days or longer has become "tainted." Most potential buyers and their agents have already seen it and dismissed it, so it is extremely difficult to convince them to give the home a second chance, even though it would be offered at a substantially lower price.

Your guide should explain the benefits of using a real estate professional to remarket their property. Reveal how you, the agent, do the following:

- Analyze why the property did not sell previously so the sellers can avoid the same mistakes this time around
- Help make the property seem fresh and new despite having been previously exposed to the market
- Properly price the property so that the listing doesn't expire again
- Make suggestions for professionally staging the property so that the interior shows the best way it possibly can to potential buyers
- Offer ideas for making the exterior of the house as attractive as possible
- Give creative tips for landscaping that makes the house look vital and attractive
- Develop a targeted marketing plan that attracts the most likely buyers to the property
- Suggest possible incentives for agents to bring buyers to look at the property

Also in your guide, provide appropriate newspaper and magazine articles about the importance of home staging and properly pricing the house for sale. These articles will tell the seller what he or she needs to know without you having to say it.

It often helps sell your value if you explain that there are three keys to selling a property with an expired listing. First, the property must be priced aggressively so as many potential buyers as possible are encouraged to view it for the first or second time. Next, you must develop ways to make the property seem new and exciting on the market with creative staging, painting, landscaping, and more. And third, the owner must offer additional incentives to agents to bring their buyers to view the house, such as a higher commission, a trip to Hawaii, or some other perk.

11) EDUCATE FOR-SALE-BY-OWNERS ABOUT WHAT THEIR INEXPERIENCE COSTS THEM

Again, the National Association of REALTORS® (NAR) statistics reveal that FSBO properties sell for 16 percent *less* than similar houses sold by REALTORS® (the official title of the members of NAR). So instead of saving the 6 percent they would pay you and the selling agent, these sellers are really losing 10 percent by trying to sell it themselves. Consider putting together a For-Sale-by-Owner Guide, which explains the benefits of using a real estate professional rather than going it alone.

Your guide should explain the services you provide, including the following:

- Accurately pricing the property for sale. I've found that, more often than not, the houses that didn't sell were incorrectly priced in the first place. A different dollar sticker can bring about remarkable results.

- Widely marketing the property to potential buyers. When you "cast a larger net, you catch more fish." When you have more buyers, you will sell the house faster and for more money. Most people think real estate professionals only advertise in the local newspaper or the REALTORS® Multiple Listing Service. However, as you know, you will actually do anything to target your marketing so that you attract the most likely buyers and their agents.
- Marketing to other real estate agents. Studies show that doing this brings in more potential buyers because a large percent of them use a real estate agent to find the right property. Experienced agents even maintain a database of agents who represent the buyers in their area.
- Making sure the buyer is qualified to purchase the property. Many people who look at FSBO properties have poor credit and recent bankruptcies, and they hope that the guy selling his own house will overlook these little facts.
- Helping clients make sure that disclosures are complied with by the sellers so they meet the legal requirements in your state.

It is very important to provide FSBOs with articles from your local newspaper real estate section about the pitfalls of trying to sell their own houses. They think they're getting a good deal, but the old saying of lawyers—"he who represents himself has a fool for a client"—holds true here, too. And the problem is, these people don't know how much they don't know, so they aren't really aware of how much their lack of expertise is costing them.

The point of this guide is to show the FSBO how much work is really involved in the marketing of a house. Once she sees the sheer volume of the paperwork required, she might not want to go it alone.

Recognize that most for-sale-by-owners are not going to list with any real estate agent during the first three to four weeks that their property is on the market. They're still "new and green" at this point and pretty convinced that they don't need you. All they're interested in is the commission, which they don't believe you earn. After a few weeks have passed, however, and they're starting to get hungry, you can begin a campaign of regular weekly mailings reminding them about the benefits of using a professional. Perhaps it has begun to occur to them that this wasn't such a good idea after all, and they're in more of a listening mode now.

Getting FSBOs to list with you takes persistence. While the average agent gives up trying to entice them into the fold after the first week, you should keep your hand in the game long after that. Most FSBOs are likely to list with an agent only after 6 to 10 weeks go by. If you are the agent who stays in regular contact with the owner, guess whom he will call when he's finally had enough.

12) MANAGE THE EMOTIONAL ASPECTS OF REAL ESTATE

Buying or selling property is one of the most emotional transactions anyone can go through because a house is not only the biggest asset most people own, but also a lot of feelings are locked up in a real estate transaction. For buyers, this is a place where they will raise their children, an oasis where they can escape from the cares of the world. In addition, this is probably their biggest investment. For sellers, the house they are leaving behind holds many fond memories, which can all trigger strong emotions.

Because this is such an emotional transaction, we must learn to manage the emotions that surround it. If a seller is emotionally attached to his "house," he will be reluctant to sell it, so you want to help him contain his feelings and separate them from this building. On the other hand, the buyer needs to become emotionally attached to her new "home" if she is going to overcome her reluctance to make such a large purchase. It is to her benefit if you can help her open up to the warm and fuzzy feelings she associates with owning a home. You can see how just a slight change in terminology alters the entire tone of a conversation.

We must help our clients realize that the past only exists in our imaginations. They must live in the present and look forward to the future. Every minute they spend in the past keeps them from living life in the present and building a wonderful future.

One way to help clients move beyond the past is by using affirmations: phrases they can repeat to themselves as a reminder to look forward to a change. Here are several you might suggest to your clients who are stuck:

- To see the future I must lift my eyes from the past.
- There is no future in the past.
- I will always treasure the memories, but I must live in the present and look forward to the future.

Another way to manage the emotional aspects of real estate is to learn what actions can trigger negative emotions. For instance, if you put up the "For Sale" sign right after a client signs the listing agreement, she is more likely to be struck by *seller's remorse* than if you wait a few days for the finality of her actions to sink in.

The other way negative emotions arise in a transaction is from *trigger words*. Certain words make sellers more attached to the property or cause a fear of moving out. Other words create fear in buyers about making a commitment or a mistake.

The following are examples of trigger words:

- *Trigger word:* sell ("When I *sell* your house…")
  Safe alternatives: convey, transfer
- *Trigger word:* buy ("When you *buy* this house…")
  Safe alternatives: purchase, own
- *Trigger word:* sign ("Please *sign* the contract.")
  Safe alternatives: ratify, autograph
- *Trigger word:* contract ("Please ratify the *contract.*")
  Safe alternatives: agreement, paperwork
- *Trigger word:* payment ("Your monthly *payment* will be…")
  Safe alternatives: investment, obligation
- *Trigger word:* home (To seller: "When I sell your *home…*")
  Safe alternatives: house, property

On the other hand, you can make trigger words work for you to bring your clients to the decision they really ought to make. For example, sellers do not want to lose a qualified buyer. Using the words *lose* or *walk away* can motivate them to sign a purchase agreement because those words bring up loss, and buyers do not ever want to think of themselves as "losers." Sample trigger words to put a deal together could be *forfeit* or *waste.* In both of these cases, you can see how just a slight change in terminology alters the entire tone of a conversation.

13) START A "TO-DON'T" LIST FOR YOURSELF

If you waste your time with clients who aren't serious, motivated, or loyal it leaves less time to work for those who are. To provide superior service to your best clients you must eliminate time-wasting activities from your business.

Everyone has made a to-do list at one time or another, but few people have ever written a "to-don't" list. Yet, the most successful people have a list of things they are going to *stop* doing—things that waste their time or energy. In other words, what should you stop doing that would make you more productive and valuable to your clients?

Some of the points you might want to consider for your list include the following:

- Don't work with unmotivated buyers because they will suck the lifeblood out of your business.
- Don't work with unqualified buyers; these are the people waiting to hit the lottery before they can afford the down payment.
- Don't work with sellers who think their two-bedroom, one-bath house is the Hearst Castle.
- Don't work with sellers whose houses are infested by termites, yet they still want top dollar.
- Don't let your business be limited by other agents' limited thinking, especially if these are the people pulling down a whopping $12,000 a year.
- Don't hang around with negative people who can brighten any room simply by leaving it.
- Don't hang around with unsuccessful people. They will not pass on to you a winning mentality.
- Don't work with sellers or buyers who don't respect your boundaries. Having your boundaries violated over and over will wear you out.
- Don't work with buyers who won't sign a Buyer-Broker Agreement with you.
- Don't stop adding to your to-don't list.

Just like a to-do list, your to-don't list should be prioritized. Which things should you stop doing immediately that would have the most positive impact on your business?

14) RELATE YOUR VALUE TO SOMETHING CLIENTS CAN UNDERSTAND

The only time people question the value of a service is when they really can't see what it's worth to them. Since buying or selling a house is a relatively rare occurrence, sometimes it helps to relate your real estate services to something they're more familiar with. Here are a few analogies you can use, depending on the lifestyle of your clients:

- Car analogy: I point to the car that the person is driving. It's often something high-end like a Lexus or a Mercedes. "You could drive a car that costs under $20,000," I say. "What made you go out and purchase an $80,000 automobile? You could buy something much less expensive and it will get you where you want to go." The client usually tells me the car is more reliable or more comfortable or safer. Whatever the benefit, he is clearly saying that it's worth paying for. Then I explain that when it comes to agents, you also get what you pay for. There are the high-end agents who offer all the bells and whistles, and there are the low-end agents who just do the basics. I then say, "I think you'll find that the ride with me will be much smoother and safer." He usually gets the picture. Obviously, if he drives a used Yugo I would have to come up with a different analogy . . . or client.
- Haircut analogy: Some people obviously spend a great deal of money on personal appearance. I will explain that my fee is higher than average because agents are like haircutters. Some haircutters give $100 haircuts and some give $20 haircuts. Both wield sharp instruments and can do a lot of damage if they are not skillful at their craft. Then I say, "I'm the kind of person who repairs $20 haircuts. If you want the job done right the first time, I'm your guy."
- Brain surgery analogy: For analytical clients, I explain it this way: "If you needed a delicate brain surgery, would you want the cheapest surgeon? Are you going to take a chance with

something that important? Obviously, you'd want the best because brain surgery is a dangerous operation requiring great skill and experience. Selling or buying a house is one of the most complex transactions in which you are ever going to be involved, and it also requires great skill and experience. If you wouldn't want brain surgery on the cheap, then you also wouldn't want a cut-rate real estate agent."

15) CONSIDER ACTING AS AN EXPERT WITNESS IN COURT

Real estate is a very complex profession filled with legal issues and pitfalls. Clients want someone who can competently and confidently guide them through the transaction while minimizing their liability. This is certainly not to say we replace or do the job of attorneys, but we must understand the law as it relates to real estate.

If you have a few years of experience under your belt and a specific area of expertise, you may be able to act as an expert witness in real estate court cases. This requires that you learn to conduct research and possibly testify in court on various areas of real estate.

Being an expert witness will increase your experience and credibility, as well as raise your confidence level, which will help you sell your value to your clients. While conducting research, you are bound to pick up information that will, some day, keep them out of trouble in dicey or problematic transactions. Knowing you will have to testify in court also forces you to stay current on various legal developments in and out of your area of interest. Don't forget to list this job prominently on your resume as there are few agents who have acted in this capacity. Nothing shouts "expert" faster than saying you sat on a witness stand under oath for a fee.

Another benefit of taking on this interesting job is that you can make many lucrative contacts in the legal community. Not only can attorneys be great resources for your clients but they can refer business to you as well. Over the years, I've received many client referrals from lawyers for whom I have acted as an expert witness because there's a built-in level of trust in my expertise. Don't forget to refer clients to the attorneys who have given you business; it maintains the goodwill as well as keeps you in the forefront of their minds.

A final bonus is that being an expert witness can provide a fairly regular source of income once you become known among real estate attorneys. I believe more people abandon our profession because of the unevenness of the income stream than because they aren't successful overall. They just can't handle the months when there's little or no money coming in. Becoming an expert witness can be a valuable revenue source that evens out the highs and lows of your cash flow, enabling you to focus on serving your clients, not your next meal.

And let's not forget how interesting the job can be. Real estate expert witnesses research unique real estate topics such as agency, disclosure, ethics, trust fund management, practice, and more. I have been one for over 20 years and have found it both intellectually stimulating and rewarding. Your clients benefit as well from an agent who remains excited about the profession rather than one who becomes burnt out.

To get started, list your experience and expertise with an expert witness directory, which can be found with an Internet search. Naturally, it helps if you have written and published a couple of articles or books on your area of expertise. Attorneys regularly refer to these directories to find qualified industry professionals who will do research and possibly testify in court. You can also contact real estate attorneys directly to let them know of your interest and availability as a paid expert on their behalf.

One good reference for real estate agents who want to act as expert witnesses is *The Expert Witness Handbook: Tips and Techniques for the Litigation Consultant* by Dan Poynter (Para Publishing, 2004). In addition, there are many other books available on this subject.

16) BECOME A REALTOR®

Every buyer and seller of real estate wants to work with an agent who is professional and ethical. REALTORS® subscribe to a strict code of ethics and are expected to maintain a higher level of knowledge of the process of buying and selling real estate. According to the National Association of REALTORS® website (www.realtor.org), an independent survey reports that 84 percent of home buyers would use the same REALTORS® again.

However, not everyone who hangs out a real estate shingle is officially a REALTOR®. You have to become a member of the National Association of REALTORS® (NAR) to use that title legally. Joining the organization is one of the most basic steps in providing value to your clients. This is the largest trade association in America, and it can help you keep in step with the latest legal, technological, and business developments in our profession. NAR also provides tools such as prewritten newsletters and regular news alerts for members.

Once you become a REALTOR®, you will be entitled to join your local board of REALTORS®. This will bring you in contact with other professionals who can give you referrals, ideas, and advice. Real estate can be a lonely business, and the agents you meet at the board will probably become your friends and allies for a lifetime.

Many agents mistakenly believe that others who belong to their local board are *their* competitors, when just the opposite is true. Sellers need agents with buyers and vice versa. Most homes, statistics reveal, are sold to buyers represented by agents. The long and the short of it is that you all need each other. What could be better than an organization that brings you together?

In addition, NAR holds an annual national convention where you can meet *agents* from across the country, see the latest products and services at their trade show to improve your business, and listen to some of the best real estate trainers and educators in the country. Meeting agents from outside your area will expand your referral base. The trade show will expose you to tools that increase your productivity and reduce your liability, and nationally known speakers will give you ideas that will spark your imagination and creativity.

Another benefit of membership in the National Association of REALTORS® is the magazine it publishes for members. In it you will find articles on the latest developments and changes in the real estate industry. You'll also expose yourself to a diversity of ideas about how agents and brokers around the nation are taking advantage of new developments and dealing with the challenges in our profession.

Many other resources are available to you as a member of NAR, including *online* education, products and services specifically for REALTORS®, marketing kits, newsletter templates, and other benefits too numerous to mention. Check out everything that's available to you at the National Association of REALTOR® website, www.realtor. com.

17) SERVE ON A COMMITTEE AT YOUR LOCAL BOARD

Serving on a committee at your local board of REALTORS® can expand your knowledge in such areas as finance, marketing, real estate law, and politics, as well as bring you into contact with other knowledgeable agents. This information and these relationships can greatly benefit your clients and increase your value.

Once you join the National Association of REALTORS® and your local board, you'll learn about all the committees that could use your service and from which you will benefit as well. Not only will you become familiar with the inner workings of your board, you'll also come into contact with some of its top agents who also share a desire to serve. Here are just a few of the more common local board committees and a general description of their usual scope of duties:

> **Awards and Recognition:** Recommends new recognitions to the board of directors and determines selection criteria for winners. Maintains plaques listing annual award winners and

chooses the physical awards for outstanding members of the local board.

Budget and Finance: Makes recommendations to the board of directors regarding all financial matters, including local board dues, fees, expenditures, and so on.

Commercial Forum: Deals with all aspects of commercial real estate, from the multiple listing service through the education of agents and brokers regarding issues of interest to the group. This is especially important to agents who have clients interested in selling or buying commercial real estate.

Commercial MLS: Maintains commercial categories within the multiple listing service system and makes recommendations to the board of directors regarding commercial MLS rules. This is of special interest to agents who sell or are interested in selling commercial real estate.

Fair Housing: Responsible for the oversight of the principles of fair housing. The duties include promotion of, and compliance with, the ideals and objectives of fair housing for all clients.

Grievance: Reviews alleged violations of the Code of Ethics and/or requests for arbitration. It either dismisses cases or forwards them to the professional standards committee for hearing.

Leadership Development: Helps prepare members for leadership positions at the local, state, and national levels.

Legislative: Screens political candidates and pursues a proactive approach to effecting proposed legislation that is of concern to members. It maintains current relationships and builds new ones at the local, state, and national level. It actively encourages current and future membership involvement in political and legislative affairs. It helps keep you aware of political developments that may affect your clients.

MLS: Sets and maintains rules for the multiple listing service. It assures smooth operations of the service, as well as soliciting suggestions for improvement and overseeing changes to the service.

New Professionals: Responsible for orienting new agents to the local board and providing new agent training.

Nominating: Nominates members for the board of directors.

Professional Development: Responsible for providing education that is beneficial to the members. It solicits suggestions for new courses and classes as well as obtains appropriate providers. It makes sure that members receive education necessary to best serve clients.

Professional Standards: Maintains high standards of professional conduct for all members and their clients.

Public Relations: Promotes the interests of local members to the public through various media outlets such as local newspaper, radio, cable television, broadcast television, magazines, and other media.

REALTORS® Political Action Committee (RPAC): The goal of the RPAC is to establish the real estate industry as a concerned, involved, political constituency. RPACs generally raise voluntary funds from local association members for use in issues, campaigns, and campaign contributions to political candidates at the federal, state, and local levels.

18) LEARN TO USE TECHNOLOGY TO ITS FULLEST

It's not enough to just create documents and do your listing presentations on a computer or receive and send email. You must learn to use technology to its fullest advantage because clients expect it these days. Once you master it, you can then go beyond the usual to increase your value.

A personal digital assistant (PDA) is essential to keep track of your appointments and contacts. Make sure that you can synchronize it with your laptop so you'll have all your valuable information backed up. Some PDAs are combined with a cell phone so you don't have to carry two separate devices. The bad news is that if you lose your cell phone, you also lose your PDA and vice versa. The same is true if one or the other breaks—you lose the use of both. However, technology is getting so reliable these days that this would be a rare event. Go beyond the ordinary to make sure you contact your clients on a regular basis, even if they want a call at 2:37 P.M. every Tuesday afternoon. Contact management software like Top Producer®, ACT!, Goldmine, or Access makes it possible.

Today, a cellular telephone is more than a phone. Most can send text messages, instant messages (IM), and even take digital photos. Use this to send pictures to buyers of properties they might be interested in even if they're not for sale. This gives you and them a clearer idea of what they want, speeding up the buying process.

Take a class that teaches you how to use all the features of your software. You'd be surprised how much you can learn and how few technological capabilities you probably use now. At a minimum, master the Microsoft Office Suite, which includes Word, Access, PowerPoint, and Excel. I use Microsoft FrontPage to make sample Web pages for prospective sellers, and Microsoft Publisher for making sample flyers. Once you learn these, then begin to learn more real estate–specific tools such as Top Producer®, Agent Office, Prep Software, and others.

Your local board of REALTORS® probably offers classes in how to use their multiple listing service, which lets you produce competitive market analyses and compile other data for clients. You should be able to email listings to your clients quite easily, not to mention send information to other agents about your listings.

If you find yourself befuddled when installing, using, or repairing software and *hardware,* simply find yourself a teenage kid. Step outside onto the sidewalk and you'll likely run head-on into a 16-year-old on a skateboard who can help you out in no time. You need to have one or more technicians available at all times who know your computer and software, because technology has a nasty habit of not working at the most inopportune moments.

Hardware that you may want to consider would be a digital camera, scanner, and color printer. An AirCard® will enable you to connect your laptop to the Internet anywhere you can get a cell signal, enabling you to look up property information for clients while sitting in front of the house. The AirCard® will also allow you to send and receive email, surf the Web, and do anything you could do with a landline connection.

Your office may have a network of equipment that you can use simply by plugging your laptop into one of its nodes. Ask other professionals about the kind of training available for operating all the equipment.

Make sure your website is regularly updated and ranks high with the search engines. Hire an expert in search engine optimization to assist you in assuring that the prospects who need your services are able to find you easily.

While you ought to appreciate the ways that technology can improve your productivity, you should never use it as a crutch or excuse to avoid talking to your clients face-to-face. Technology is only a tool; real estate is still about building relationships with people.

19) BUILD RAPPORT WITH YOUR CLIENTS

People buy and sell through people they like. Before you work with a buyer, seller, FSBO, or expired listing, find something you both have in common because that helps you instantly build a rapport. Ask buyers about their hobbies, movies they like, activities they engage in, charities they support, or any other interests you might share. Look around the client's house for signs of anything you might have in common such as diplomas, awards, and trophies.

The first words out of your mouth when you initially meet a client should not be about you, but about them. Take a sincere interest in them immediately. There's an old saying: "People don't care how much you know, until they know how much you care."

Let clients also see your humanity, not just your business side. Talk about your family, hobbies, education, charitable activities, and other outside interests. Probably the only subjects that are taboo are the usual: politics, sex, and religion.

This commonality helps to humanize you and shows your value, not only as a real estate professional but as a person as well. Do not start any presentation before a rapport has been built. How do you know if you have accomplished this goal? They're the ones who will bring up the subject of real estate, not you.

Another way to build and increase the depth of a rapport is to "pace" potential clients. Essentially, this means to mirror them. Pay attention to how they talk and move, to their mannerisms, their energy, body language, and in general how they express themselves, and then mirror the same back. This makes them instantly feel as if you are their kind of people, as if they've known you all their lives and you are someone they can invite into their living room. Be careful, however, not to let it look as if you are mimicking them; you have to be subtle.

Start by noting and matching how loud a person's voice is when he talks. Someone who speaks softly will relate better to another person who also speaks softly. Likewise, someone who speaks more loudly will usually feel more comfortable if you talk at the same level. Pacing often includes matching the other person's rate of speech. If she speaks more quickly than average, you'll want to talk a bit faster. Slow your speech for those who communicate at a more leisurely pace. You can see that not matching rate or volume of speech could actually create lack of communication and a lack of rapport between two parties.

Besides speech, another attribute to note at the very outset is the potential client's energy level. Some people are naturally very high-energy and frenetic while others are lower energy and reserved.

Make a conscious effort to pace the other party and you'll find that a rapport builds much more rapidly.

The best way to build rapport with clients is to be yourself. This doesn't mean that you drop all boundaries or bare your soul. Of course you have to keep appropriate professional boundaries, and you can learn what these are by paying attention to the social standards in your area. In the Midwest, for example, people are a little more folksy. They might offer you a bowl of Jell-O with marshmallows in it and show you pictures of their kids. On the East Coast, people tend to be more reserved. However, given these limitations, you can still reveal your true nature. If you are a warm person, be warm. If you are more formal, don't try to crack jokes and hug people because you probably can't pull it off for long. People will see right through you and then you will lose all your credibility. In the end, your real traits are your best traits. If a client really doesn't accept you for who you are, find people who are more compatible with you. Don't try to force the two of you to fit if it doesn't come naturally.

Another mistake people make is trying to be perfect. Don't bother; clients know that you aren't because no one is. When I first started in this profession over 30 years ago, I thought the way I would differentiate myself from all the other agents in my area was to promise "the perfect real estate transaction." Is that dumb or is that dumb?

It put me under tremendous pressure to live up to the impossible standard I had set for myself. In less than a year I had developed an ulcer. The final straw came about when, in the front seat of my car, I told some new buyers that I would give them a perfect transaction. Then I pulled out of the driveway and promptly turned in the wrong direction!

You are better off making promises you can deliver than making glittering promises that you can't keep. Nothing ruins a relationship faster than a series of broken promises. After that incident, I told all my clients that this is not a perfect business and that things do go wrong. However, my job was to deal with all of the challenges for them and make everything go as smoothly as possible. This was a promise they could believe and appreciate. As a result, my value in the eyes of my clients went up immeasurably.

I believe that what makes us comfortable with our friends is that we can be ourselves without pretending to be someone we aren't. Shouldn't we have the same kind of relationship with our clients? In fact, almost all of my clients eventually become my friends. I have gone skiing, sailing, hiking, and biking with them. I know many brokers believe we shouldn't mix business and pleasure, but in my opinion, this business should be pleasurable and if we genuinely like our clients, why shouldn't we enjoy their company during our off-hours?

20) PROVIDE INFORMATION, NOT JUST DATA

Today, data is available everywhere. There's so much of it that people are becoming overwhelmed and overloaded. The problem when too much data is available is that it causes the mind to shut down. We fall into "analysis paralysis" and fail to take action that is in our best interests. It is well documented that people make better decisions when they have less information, as long as the information is pertinent. When we are allowed to operate without being inundated, it enables rapid cognition; that is, it lets us easily sort through the data and notice what is significant. Extra information confuses us. It forces us to muddle through the data, rather than focus on the business at hand. One way of looking at this is to ask yourself, "If I had to figure out what kind of bug spray to use to keep the aphids out of my garden, do I want to read an entire encyclopedia, or do I want to peruse a one-page pamphlet?"

If all we do as agents is provide data, we are simply adding to the avalanche of details and competing with other data sources such as the Internet, title companies, and county recorders. We need to differentiate ourselves from these other service providers.

On the other hand, we do need to provide appropriate information, which is data that is usable to the client, because we have sifted and customized it specifically for them. For example, there are probably thousands of homes currently on the market in your area. That's raw data. Taking the time to learn that your clients want a three-bedroom, two-and-a-half-bath house with two stories and a view in a certain price range, will narrow that raw data down to just a few homes. Turning data into information saves your clients time, visibly demonstrates your expertise, and illuminates your value to them. You've just done a lot of work so they don't have to.

Another example of data is student performance scores in local schools. There are many sources for these numbers, but knowing that your clients have two children, in the third and fifth grades, allows you to provide only the information that is applicable to them. It allows them to make an informed decision about which school district they want to choose to buy a home in without doing a lot of footwork.

There are thousands of homes on the market, so part of the agent's job is to funnel the appropriate information to the clients. First, of course, the agent has to understand what her client's needs are so she funnels the right data. Then she has to go out and sift all the data until she comes up with only what the client needs to know. There are a lot of houses on the market, but the client is only interested in ones that are comparable to hers. What do you use to filter all the data so you present only the properties that fall within that particular client's range? For the most part, the filters can be broken down into location, price, type of architecture, size, school system, access to transportation, and other amenities. Your expertise can help the client sort out the superfluous data from the valuable information.

Buying or selling a home is a complex transaction involving hundreds of steps and almost as many pages of documentation. You can make it easier by helping your clients recognize which elements apply to them and which do not. So don't be a data provider, be an information resource. Use your expertise and experience to learn everything you need to know about your clients so you can give them just the material that applies to them—and no more.

21) MAINTAIN A CURRENT LIST OF YOUR CLIENTS

Some agents are individual brokers, some are brokers who work under other brokers, and some are salespeople. You may work with a hundred other agents or only a handful. Whichever situation you are in, you will want to retire someday. Or you might just want to move out of the area or change careers. When that time comes you only have one thing of real value to sell: your client list. Every agent, whether working in a big or small firm, should have built up their own client list. You may not technically own the list, but you can "own" the clients if you've spent time over the years cultivating a real relationship with them.

Many agents hope that someday they can own a large real estate brokerage. They believe they'll start making all the money everyone seems to think they already make. I used to think that way—until I achieved my dream. Then I found out about the reality of paying the bills month in and month out whether the company was generating an income or not. In the end, when I decided to sell, it turned out that the only thing I had that was truly of value was my list of clients. When the day came to move on, I realized I was in the same position as an individual agent. Of all those "assets" that were supposed to be so priceless, none of them was worth much when it came time to sell. That all-important list was the one treasure I really possessed.

As a broker, I am well aware that all my other assets aren't a big selling point to another broker when I am trying to sell my business to him. He knows perfectly well that an office full of agents means nothing because they are all free to leave whenever they want. He has absolutely no claim on these people. And the office location might be golden, but so what? Anyone can find the same kind of location for the cost of first and last months' rent. Even the franchise name that we paid so much for could be purchased by someone else for the same price we paid, possibly even less. That list of clients was the single possession that was worth anything because it was the only thing a new broker or agent coming into my area could not duplicate overnight.

Because this list is computerized, once you sell it, it is simple to send a letter to the people in your own database announcing the passing of the torch. You can say something like, "Dear xxxxx, I want to thank you for your business and your friendship over the years. However, it's now time for me to (retire, move, etc.). I am entrusting you to another fine agent, xxxxx, who I know will show you the same diligent and friendly service that I have provided. I hope you will show him/her your loyalty as he/she is very similar to me in many respects. Please feel free to call me at any time if you have questions or require additional information about this transition. Your new agent will be in touch with you over the next few weeks to introduce him/herself. Sincerely, xxxxx."

Buying your list of clients is a great benefit to any agent because it will help him quickly establish a business in a new area. In addition, it can provide you with a stream of income for many years to come, depending on how you structure the sale of your list. You cannot overestimate its value now and in the future.

So if you don't have a list, start today. Go back through your old escrow files and put your client information into some contact management software database such as ACT!, Microsoft Access, Goldmine, Top Producer®, or another similar program. To have value to a future purchaser, your list must be current, computerized, and detailed.

The more detail you have on your clients, the more valuable your list, because it gives the new agent more opportunities for rapport and marketing. Some of the data you might want to collect over the years could include the following:

- Names of husband, wife, children, pets
- Occupations of husband and wife
- Birthdates of all family members
- Significant dates such as closing date of property or anniversaries
- Hobbies and other interests

- Favorite foods, wines, books, and movies
- Pet types and names

All of this gives the buyer a window into these people's lives so he isn't starting out cold. Don't forget that the names alone don't ensure that the new agent will automatically pick these people up as clients. They might not be so eager to be handed over to somebody new, after all, and they could have other ideas about where to take their business after you leave. Including all this personal information gives the new agent a chance to hit the ground running with your past clients.

In addition to being a valuable asset to sell at some point in the future, the very act of compiling the list is good for your business. It gives you reasons to stay in touch on a regular basis, which you can accomplish by sending birthday cards, anniversary reminders, and more.

If you do decide to sell your list, however, make sure that the new agent is similar to you in temperament and communication style. Your clients enjoy working with you because you are similar to them in certain ways. If their next agent is like you as well, there's a good chance they will be loyal to him or her.

22) CREATE A SENSE OF URGENCY

If you really want to be of service to your clients, give them deadlines to help them come to quick decisions about the action they need to take. Whenever a person has forever to make a decision, she will pretty much take forever. A deadline is usually the soonest she will do anything. Deadlines are powerful, then, because they cause people to take action.

But the key to creating a sense of urgency is not to just impose some arbitrary deadline on your clients, because their tendency will just be to resist it. The trick is to give them a cutoff date in a way that makes them believe it was their idea. For instance, say to the buyer,

"You said you have three months left on your lease. Is that when you want to move in, or is it earlier?" I once said to a seller, "If I recall, your first grandchild is due in February. Would you like to be relocated near her by then?"

If sellers tell you they need to paint or landscape before they list their house with you, simply say, "So, how long do you think you'll need to do the work?" Get them to think about it and make a commitment. If they reply, "About three weeks," you can respond, "Terrific! Let's list the property today and we won't put it into the MLS for three weeks." This accomplishes two very important goals. First, you let them establish a deadline, and in my experience, a deadline is the soonest anyone will do anything. Second, you have just gotten the listing. I've found that if you leave without the listing, the chances of getting it later are slim.

Be aware that, to avoid making a commitment, sellers will use all kinds of delaying tactics, such as the following:

- "I need to talk to my accountant, attorney, or financial planner."
- "My neighbor said he wanted to buy my house."
- "I want to do some painting and carpeting."
- "We need to find another house before we put this one on the market."

You can use a similar tactic to get a buyer to move forward. If she tells you she needs to talk with a lender before making an offer, just reply, "Great, when would you want to schedule the appointment? I know several loan brokers I think you would really like." The following are other typical delaying tactics of buyers:

- "I need to talk to my landlord."
- "I need to talk to my accountant."
- "I have to talk with my wife."

In all of these cases, take what was meant to be a delaying tactic and use it as motivator.

23) DO WHAT YOU DO BEST, HIRE OUT THE REST

To maximize your value you must spend the majority of your time doing what you do best—talking face-to-face with clients. If you throw your real skills away by wasting time on paperwork, flyers, or office cleaning, you are not exactly maximizing your value. The only job that directly generates income is spending one-on-one time with clients. This is the money task. Any of the back-office tasks may be necessary for the business, but in the end, you will lose money if you try to do them all yourself.

Any time someone else can do a job as well or better than you, for the same or less money than you, then it's to your advantage to pay the person to do it for you. I've heard people complain that they can't afford it and I respond, "You can't afford not to do it because their time is tax deductible and yours isn't."

The Internal Revenue Service does not allow you to deduct your own time from your taxable income, even though it is spent on your business, because it's very hard to establish a value for it. We all think our time is worth a great deal of money, but the IRS would beg to differ, so to avoid any disputes, they just don't permit an allowance for what you yourself do. On the other hand, if you hire someone to do the work for you, the time immediately becomes tax deductible.

If you find menial tasks eating away too much of your time (and you know this is happening because you haven't seen a client for a week), consider hiring an assistant. Hiring one isn't nearly as expensive as you might think. Remember that most agents are in at least a 40 percent federal tax bracket (income plus self-employment tax) plus state taxes, as applicable. This is fairly high, and the higher the bracket, the more you need deductions. It all comes down to this: you either pay an assistant to make your life easier or you can pay the IRS, and help pay for a bridge to nowhere in Alaska.

Look at it this way. Let's say you are paying the assistant $20 an hour. It isn't really $20 an hour because you can use the salary as a deduction. If you are in a 50 percent tax bracket, the net cost to you is now $10 an hour. For $10 an hour, isn't it worth it to you to unload all the work you don't want to do, and dedicate your time to your real job? (See Tip #101 for more details on assistants.)

Any time you are about to engage in an activity that takes you away from either prospecting or making presentations to clients, ask yourself, "Could I hire someone to do this job?" If someone else can do the job just as well as you, go ahead and hire her. And don't forget that she can probably do the job faster and better than you because it's what she does for a living.

One of the most common jobs real estate agents do themselves is their taxes. This is, unequivocally, a bad idea. The tax code is infamously long and complicated, and it changes endlessly. Unless you want to switch jobs and prepare taxes for a living, don't even think about spending all the time it takes to do your own taxes. Few sources can liberate you from your money faster than the IRS.

Marketing, making flyers, developing and maintaining a website—all these and other jobs can turn out to be a black hole that sucks in your available time. You might even enjoy some of these activities. I've heard people say this over the years, and I know that's how they are lured in. My response is "Fine. Make the flyers yourself. Just count the time as leisure hours. Let it cut into your free time if you love it so much. Just don't call it work, because it isn't making you money."

24) ANTICIPATE QUESTIONS IN ADVANCE

How often have you visited your doctor's office, left to walk to your car, and found that you hadn't asked him half the questions you had in mind that morning? It is not uncommon for people to show up for a meeting with a professional and feel overwhelmed. They haven't made up a list of questions to ask, so they get carried along by the conversation and forget what they wanted to know. You can help new prospects by anticipating the questions they might ask and then having the answers ready. You are basically compensating for the fact that they either forget the questions, or they didn't know them in the first place.

Questions give the prospect a chance to examine the entire process of home buying or selling. In order for it to work, you have to be on the lookout for what clients might be implying, but not saying outright. You can often tell with one question that there's another one they should be asking, but didn't; ask it for them. Also think about what they might not know enough to ask about. People who are really just beginning genuinely aren't aware of how much they don't know. And finally, what are they afraid to ask? You can see how helpful you will be to your clients if you take this approach.

Use your experience to come up with the most common issues buyers and sellers have before they begin the transaction. When your questions reflect what's in their minds, you look like a genius! Or at least a mind reader. Actually, it's not really all that hard. All you have to do is put yourself in the place of a buyer or seller and ask yourself, "What would I want to know about this transaction?" Then prepare answers to the questions by asking more experienced agents how they would deal with them.

For example, if you were a buyer, especially a first-time one, you'd probably want to   know the following:

- What's the process of buying a home?
- How does home financing work?
- What's in a purchase agreement?
- Can I back out once I sign the purchase agreement?
- How do I know the house is free from construction defects?
- How do I know the house is free from pests?
- What steps must I take to fulfill the terms of the contract?
- When is the down payment due?

- How long will it take me to buy a house?
- When can I move in?
- How do I transfer utilities into my name?
- How do I deduct the mortgage interest and property tax from my income taxes?

If you were a first-time seller you would likely want to know the following:

- What's the process of selling my house?
- What can I personally do to help it sell for the most money?
- What do I say to prospective buyers?
- How can I defer tax on the gain from the sale of my house?
- How long will the whole process take?
- Do I really need to put a "For Sale" sign on my property?
- Do I really need to put a lockbox on my property?
- What costs will I incur in the sale of my house?
- What are the tax consequences?
- What can I do if my house is worth less than what I owe on it?

An owner whose listing has expired and is considering relisting might ask the following questions:

- Where were you when my house was on the market?
- Why didn't my house sell?
- What will you do differently from my previous agent?
- What price should I put on my house?
- What can you do to assure me that my house will sell this time?
- Haven't all the buyers seen my house already?

An FSBO who is considering listing with you will probably ask these questions:

- What can you do that I haven't already done myself?

- Why hasn't my house sold yet?
- Will you bring a buyer for two percent?
- Will you sign an open listing?
- Would you complete the paperwork if I find a buyer on my own? And what would you charge me?
- Why should I list with you?

25) ANTICIPATE PROBLEMS IN ADVANCE

Just as you can anticipate questions from clients, you can anticipate many of the problems that will arise with a real estate transaction. More than anything, your clients want to know that you are the consummate professional and they don't have to worry about a thing. What better way to soothe their nerves than to let them know what problems will arise before they have a crisis on their hands. What better way to inspire confidence in your abilities than to show them you are so familiar with the ins and outs of the business that you can anticipate difficult predicaments now while they're still molehills. Buying and selling a house already seems like a huge mountain to climb. Why not take it down a notch?

Here are some of the most common problems that occur, along with possible solutions. Obviously, you will encounter others, so start making a list of your own.

Common Buyer Problems Listing Agents Should Anticipate

Problem: The buyer whose contract was ratified is not approved for the loan.
Solution: The listing agent should continue to market the property to obtain a backup offer.

Problem: The buyer's inspections may reveal unanticipated problems.

Solution: Listing agents should have the inspections and required work done before putting the property on the market.

Problem: There are few current comparable sales and the loan appraisal does not come in for the full purchase price of the property.
Solution: The listing agent should anticipate this situation arising and counter all offers with wording such as "Buyer to make up difference between purchase and loan appraisal (if any) in cash."

Problem: The property may not receive any offers and the seller thinks it's the listing agent's fault.
Solution: Smart listing agents warn their sellers of this possibility before the property is placed on the market. Remind them that buyers, not agents, determine the market. All we can do is our best to attract the most appropriate buyers, but we cannot guarantee who's out there at any point in time.

Problem: The property may receive many offers, so the seller thinks the price is too low and wants to raise the price.
Solution: The listing agent should alert the sellers that due to the condition of their property and your superior marketing skills, there could be a number of offers fairly early on. This does not mean that the property is underpriced. In fact, having many offers drives up the perceived value of the property and could possibly start a bidding war. If they were to raise the price, all of this competition would go away.

Problem: The buyer whose contract is ratified does not qualify for a loan.
Solution: The listing agent should make sure that every buyer who makes an offer provides a preapproval—not just a prequalification—letter from a lender, greatly increasing the chances they will qualify for a loan.

Problem: When the buyer does not qualify for a loan, all the other potential buyers have found other properties.

Solution: The listing agent should be sure that any ratified offer contains a "continue to show and accept backup offers" clause. This will enable you to continue to look for other offers, which encourages the buyer in "first-position" to move forward with his financing without delay, and keeps other potential buyers interested.

Problem: The inspections reveal unanticipated problems.

Solution: The listing agent should warn the seller in advance that the job of inspectors is to find issues that may or may not be significant. You will work with the inspector to determine which issues do and do not need to be addressed. If nothing is found, you will look like a hero. If issues are found as you predicted, you will look like a genius!

Problem: The loan approval process takes longer than expected.

Solution: Again, warn the seller in advance that this crucial aspect may take longer than anticipated because banks work on their own schedule. If the seller has critical deadlines to meet, such as scheduled moving vans, transferring funds to another transaction, and so on, see if you can negotiate leeway in advance. The sooner you make the arrangements, the more flexibility you will have.

Problem: The loan appraisal may not come in for the full purchase price of the property.

Solution: If the listing agent knows this could be a concern (in a declining or flat market), he should consider only accepting offers where the buyers have enough cash to make up the difference between the appraised price of the property and the loan amount.

Common Seller Problems Agents Representing the Buyer Should Anticipate

Problem: The loan approval process takes longer than expected.

Solution: The agent for the buyer should warn his clients in advance that this crucial aspect may take longer than anticipated because banks work on their own schedule. If the buyer has critical deadlines to meet such as scheduled moving vans, a lease coming to an end, and so on, see if you can negotiate alternatives and extensions in advance. The sooner you make the arrangements, the more flexibility you will have.

Problem: The loan appraisal may not come in for the full purchase price of the property.
Solution: If the agent for the buyer knows this could be a concern (in a declining or flat market), he should make sure his client has enough cash to make up the difference between the appraised price of the property and the loan amount.

Problem: The seller may not vacate the property as scheduled.
Solution: The agent for the buyer could negotiate a clause that requires the seller to leave a substantial amount of money in escrow as "rent" at the outset of the transaction. This amount should be high enough to make it expensive for the seller to hold over for long.

Problem: The seller may not leave personal property as promised.
Solution: The agent for the buyer could negotiate that the seller leave an amount in escrow sufficient to secure the personal property. If the property is not transferred, the buyer can use these funds to purchase similar property.

Problem: The personal property the seller leaves behind may not function properly.
Solution: The agent for the buyer should negotiate a clause that covers repairs or have the seller provide a home warranty plan that would cover this issue.

Recall all of the transactions you've had and what problems regularly occurred. You'll find they tend to happen over and over again. By looking at recurring issues, you can develop solutions before they occur, which can protect your client. If you have solutions for these issues before they come up, you will look like a genius, and it will make the transaction go a lot smoother.

26) PRACTICE ACTIVE LISTENING SKILLS

More than anything, clients want to feel heard and understood. This is especially important to them on a major transaction like real estate.

Probably the biggest factor in selling your value is superior listening skills, which will probably come as a big surprise to newer agents. In their haste to make a sale, they wrongly believe that they must talk their heads off and control the conversation. In reality, all they're doing is overwhelming the prospect and making her feel that she is invisible. This does not inspire confidence—in fact with many people, it makes them wonder if the agent isn't talking a little too much to cover up a lack of ability.

And if it is control you're after, nonstop talking will not give it to you. The fact is, the talker does not control the conversation. As most salespeople know, asking a question controls it because any time a question is asked, the other party must stop talking, think, and then respond. Asking a question has many other advantages. It brings the client into the process. When she answers it, she feels that she is making a contribution. And you are giving her the impression that you really care about what she has to say and that you want to meet her needs. All of this inspires faith and trust, and it builds considerable rapport.

However, learning active listening skills isn't as simplistic as just remembering to pause more often in conversations. Real listening isn't just stopping long enough to let the other person get a word or two in. It is an actual skill that takes time and training. While there isn't room here to give you an entire listening skills class, here are a few suggestions.

First, squarely face your clients and focus all your attention on them. This indicates that you are listening intently. Make good eye contact (unless there are indications that they are uncomfortable with it), sit upright and lean toward them, take notes as appropriate, and do not interrupt. All of this makes the other person feel that you are genuinely interested in what he has to say. People reveal a lot more to an interested party than to someone who is practically dozing off.

Reinforce your listening with nonverbal communications such as smiling, gesturing, and nodding. This shows that you are open to him as a person and avidly taking in everything he says. This also encourages him to elaborate further on his thoughts and feelings.

Next, ask questions such as who, what, when, where, how, and why. This gently encourages the client to give you as much information as possible. Follow his answers with clarifying questions that get him to expand on what he said, to go even deeper into his thinking. All of this greatly improves communication and cuts down on misunderstandings down the line.

After this, reflect on what you think you heard the client say. You can then say things that reinforce and support his thinking, which makes him feel even more secure that he chose you as his agent. Repeat facts and reflect on your own feelings to reinforce the connection between the two of you.

Active listening takes training and practice, but when clients feel fully heard they will love you for it. Here are some of the elements of active listening:

- Listen with all your senses. Don't just use your ears; use your eyes and other senses to discern unspoken thoughts, wishes, and desires.
- Acknowledge that you are listening, but you don't necessarily have to agree.
- Encourage deeper thought. Ask your clients to explain, expand, and elaborate on important thoughts so you can uncover the entire picture.

- Don't just listen to the words. Most meaning is communicated as much through body language as it is through words. Listen for feelings as well as content.
- Clarify what you have heard. Restate what your clients have said just to make sure what you think you've heard is what they believe they said.
- Monitor yourself. Be aware of your own feelings and opinions so you can see how they might prejudice what you are hearing.
- State your opinions last. If you feel you must state your views, keep them to yourself until you have heard everything your client has to say.

Providing feedback is crucial to clear communications. What someone says and what you think she said can be dramatically different. Everyone has filters, assumptions, and judgments that can distort what they hear. Repeating what you believe you heard helps to confirm and clarify that your interpretation is on track. However, don't just feed it back word for word. That doesn't verify that you really understood the words. Instead, paraphrase your understanding in your own words. If emotional issues are raised, be sure to empathize with the person to show that you understand her experience. Remember that buying or selling real estate is an extremely emotional transaction. (See Tip #12)

Here are some attitudes and actions that can block active listening:

- Bias: You may not like one-story homes and yet that's all your client seems interested in viewing. Remember, you aren't going to be living in the house he is buying. Be open to new and different ideas and don't impose your views on others.
- Distractions: Eliminate or at least reduce noise, interruptions, and other items that may divert your full attention.

- Preparing a response: Many times you may be tempted to think about a response to a statement or question before hearing out the client completely.
- "Hot button" words: Watch how you react to words that grab you emotionally. The usual tendency is to overreact.
- Watch your words: Avoid the use of "hot button" words that just seem to generate a reaction in people. Words like penalty (e.g., prepayment penalty), contract (e.g., ratify the contract), and sign (e.g., sign here) can trigger strong negative feelings.
- Filtering: Be careful how you filter your information. If, for instance, you don't care for a particular neighborhood and your clients seem to like it, listen without judgment as you would when they are discussing an area you do like.

Finally, summarize your new understanding and explain what you will do to act upon what you have heard. Nobody wants an agent who listens but doesn't follow up with action. Then ask if there are any further questions, and repeat what action you promised to take.

27) DEVELOP TRUST WITH YOUR CLIENTS

Trust is the most crucial part of your relationship with clients. If you have it, your sellers will price the property as you suggest, share important information, do the inspections and repairs you recommend, stage the property as appropriate, and follow any other suggestions you make that will help the house to sell. If you have the trust of your buyers, they will be loyal to you, share important information, and make offers when you suggest and at the price you recommend. Not only does trust build value, but it can make your business much more efficient and effective. This means that you can do a better job for everyone.

But you earn that trust by who you are as much as by what you do. If you are a person of character who possesses qualities like honesty, scrupulousness, empathy, and backbone, then the client can comfortably rely on your overall integrity. Yes, of course you could fake it, but sooner or later people will see who you really are. Once this transaction is over, will they really come back to someone whose character they don't respect? It's more likely that they'll be counting the days until they don't have to do business with the person anymore.

The problem is that many people do not trust real estate agents as a matter of course because a handful of them are unscrupulous and unethical. These are the people who get all the headlines and give the rest of us a bad name. In fact, according to the 2006 Harris Poll measuring trust of professions in America, real estate agents were at the bottom:

1. Doctors
2. Dentists
3. Nurses
4. Accountants
5. Lawyers
6. Bankers
7. Financial advisors
8. Mechanics
9. Insurance agents
10. Real estate agents

You can see that real estate agents face an uphill battle when it comes to gaining the trust of our clients. The question is "How do you develop trust?" Obviously, establishing trust takes time, but here are some ways that will help build it quickly:

- Tell the truth. Whether it's good news or bad news, be honest.
- Stay in touch. Contact your sellers and buyers on a regular basis.

- Communicate clearly.
- Listen actively (see Tip #26).
- Do what you say you're going to do.
- Under-promise and over-deliver.
- If you don't know the answer to a question just say you don't know.
- Hold sellers' interests above your own.
- Hold buyers' interests above your own.
- Be prompt for appointments.

One of the fastest ways to develop trust with clients is to educate them about the process. Remember that buying or selling a home is a very complex transaction with hundreds of steps that must be completed in the proper order or it will not close. The more people understand, the more they will trust.

28) DEVELOP A SPECIALIZATION

Top producers have a niche and they own it. You can't be all things to all people, but you can be all things to a *specific group* of people.

Having a specialization makes you an expert, which connotes the idea of authority to just about everyone. People expect to pay an authority more money than they would a novice or a generic agent. Ask yourself, "Who is paid better, a general practitioner or a brain surgeon?" If a patient has a brain tumor, the brain surgeon has much deeper knowledge in the one area that this person specifically needs. Not only does she have the same body of knowledge as the general practitioner, and attended school the same number of years, but she went the extra mile and gained her particular degree in addition to all that. The surgeon spent years more honing her knowledge in her area of specialization.

The same is true for real estate professionals. We all pass the same state licensing exam. But then some go on to specialize in purchasing commercial offices or high rise buildings, or selling dude ranches (which include everything but the dudes).

There are other ways to be a specialist. The most basic way would be to zero in on your own particular city or area. Or perhaps you sell different types of residential property such as condominiums, town houses, or cooperatives, in addition to commercial real estate like office buildings or warehouses. You could also specialize in a particular kind of transaction like tax-deferred exchanges, lease options, government-backed loans, and so on.

There are special government programs for financing, which let you help a myriad of people who never dreamed they could own their own home. They may not have a lot of money, but they are highly motivated, and there are plenty of them. If you find your niche selling in this range of property, you will never be without clients.

Some agents specialize in lower-priced starter properties, median-priced properties, or high-end luxury homes. Then, of course, there are the special needs of people who are buying for the first time, who are seniors, or who are relocating. Last, but certainly not least, you could be a leasing agent or property manager, which has the distinct advantage of offering you a steady monthly income.

Each type of property and each kind of job require different levels of experience and expertise, and investing your time and energy will pay big dividends over the long run. Wherever you live, there is most certainly an organization that offers training, and some even provide specialized designations.

It usually doesn't take long to become a specialist. You just need to commit to learning everything you can about the subject. If you spend one hour a day in focused, concentrated research on your subject, you can become an expert very quickly. Once you have a specialization, you can target buyers who need your newly developed knowledge. So if you decide to concentrate on tax-deferred exchanges, for example, you will attract people who own rental property and who want to sell it while deferring the gain into another rental property. To attract the right clients, you could hold seminars for people who own investment property.

The following are potential areas of specialization:

Geographic

- City
- County
- Neighborhood
- Subdivision

Property Type

- Condominiums
- Town homes
- Cooperatives
- Single-family starter homes
- Single-family median priced homes
- Single-family luxury homes
- Resort property
- Vacation homes
- Small income property, such as duplexes, triplexes, or fourplexes
- Large income property, such as apartment buildings
- Commercial property
- Unique properties such as churches or one-of-a-kind homes

Transaction Type

- Sales
- Leasing
- Exchanges
- Move-ups
- Move-downs
- Transfers/relocations
- Foreclosures

Client Type

- Renters
- First-time buyers
- Retirees
- Seniors
- Investors in residential real estate
- Investors in commercial real estate
- Generation X
- Multicultural clients

29) BECOME THE EXPERT IN YOUR GEOGRAPHIC AREA

You can really offer value to your clients by becoming the expert in your own geographic area. Whenever somebody wants something special, all the other agents know that you're the one to call to find it.

You can genuinely help people meet their needs because you know the area better than anyone. You know where the schools are located along with the scholastic scores of the various grade levels. (Parents care a great deal about this.) You will be familiar with the location of all the police and fire stations. You will instantly be able to rattle off the location of the shopping districts and types of transportation, including freeways, public transportation, and major thoroughfares.

Just like the beat cops in the olden days, you have to regularly walk through your neighborhood to find out who is fixing up their homes, who is buying a second home in the country, and who is buying the empty lot next to them. You would never learn any of this by driving through in your car. To really become acquainted with a place, you have to see it on foot.

Every city has great restaurants, so consider developing a list of some of the best places to eat, as well as some of the lesser known establishments. Is there anything special in the area, such as a community pool or regional theater?

How about parks, museums, or art galleries? Is your town known for anything unique? For instance, Gilroy, in central California, is famous for being the garlic capital of the world. Every year, tens of thousands of people visit the garlic festival and buy everything from garlic garlands to garlic jelly.

What are the various types of communities in your area and what is the price range of the houses? What unique amenities does each offer? Why do residents choose one community over the other?

By putting this kind of information on your website and constantly mentioning the name of your town, it will raise the ranking of your site. And anyone who is googling for information about your area because they're considering buying there, will automatically become aware of you and think about contacting you when it comes time to buy. Be sure that everything you include on your website will be very attractive to people wanting to move into your town.

Many REALTORS® get involved in their community by running for city council or the board of supervisors. These positions will not only keep them at the forefront of developments in their area, but will also give them increased visibility. And who knows where it will lead? One broker in my area who did exactly this and eventually became a U.S. congressman.

Make friends with people employed at your local building department to find out when and where new developments will be built. Become a member of your local Board of REALTORS® so you'll be let in on any information that will affect your local market. You should also talk to agents in your area about changes in zoning laws, alterations due to eminent domain, and anything else that's relevant.

30) KNOW WHAT MAKES YOU SPECIAL AS AN AGENT

If there is any one thing you want to avoid as a real estate professional, it's being considered a commodity. A commodity is a product that is easily replaced by another product. What happens when you don't stand out from the crowd is that the only factor left for consumers to mull over when deciding whether to choose you over someone else is price. You are already in an uphill battle against the tendency of people in this country to assume that all agents are alike. It's up to all of us to buck that trend.

First off, you must find your unique selling proposition (USP). For instance, you might have been a nurse or a teacher before getting into real estate. What abilities did you pick up that you can now sell to a prospect? Be creative in your thinking. Any former career gives you some kind of unique skills that other real estate agents don't possess. An ex-nurse, for example, is probably used to handling high-pressure situations; she is prepared to handle the stress and intense emotions of absolute deadlines which one encounters when closing a real estate deal. An ex-teacher knows how to educate his clients, which comes in handy in the complicated world of real estate.

Again, the point is to differentiate yourself from your competitors. What special education have you received or what experiences have you had that can benefit your clients? To take myself as an example, I obtained a broker's license, financial planning certification, and tax certification. I went through all that time and trouble because I knew that when people buy or sell a house, it impacts them in three major areas: their real estate holdings, their financial plan now and in the future, and their tax standing. There might be other factors, but these are the big three. If I didn't make myself highly qualified in these areas, I felt I might fail my clients in a major way. Yet very few real estate professionals have this combination of qualifications. The knowledge they have given me makes me unique.

What makes you unique? Why would someone choose you over other agents?

If you have not yet developed a USP, write about all the aspects of your background and describe how they make you different from other real estate professionals. Then survey your previous clients and ask one very simple question: "Why did you hire me?" Write their answers down.

Now look carefully at the two lists you have compiled. What words appear most commonly among them? These are the basis of your USP because they are what make you different from the crowd and are the reason why people hire you.

31) SEPARATE YOUR CLIENTS' NEEDS FROM THEIR WANTS

There's an old saying in real estate: "Buyers are liars and sellers are worse."

This is a pretty negative perspective and I believe it comes about because we don't listen to our clients carefully enough. At the end of three frustrating months, it might seem as if the buyer was looking at one kind of house, only to buy something totally different. But do you really think that was her intention? It may seem as if a buyer explained to you the parameters of what she wanted in a house, and then bought the opposite, but couldn't there be another explanation?

I've found that the crux of the problem is that we agents don't spend enough time helping our clients to clearly differentiate between their wants and needs. They're just too close to their emotions to do this job by themselves. This is where real estate professionals can be really helpful, by giving their clients a clear assessment of their life today and what they need from their living situation. Some people must have a slice of nature in their own backyard and they think of their home as a getaway, whereas others just want a place that is carefree and convenient.

To differentiate wants from needs, simply draw a line down the middle of a piece of paper and write *wants* on the left and *needs* on the right. Start on the left by having your clients list everything they want in their dream house—the sky's the limit. Then, test to see if any of these wants are needs by asking, "If you found a house that was otherwise perfect, but it didn't have this item, would you still buy it?" If the answer is yes, then it's a want and not a need. If the answer is no, it's a need and you would put it on the right-hand side of the paper.

Be aware, though, that this test doesn't replace the necessity to listen carefully to your clients and not make assumptions. The same amenity that is a need for one could be a want for another, and you have to listen to tell the difference. Most agents, for instance, would assume that a swimming pool is a want, but I had clients with a handicapped child who could only exercise in a pool. For this family an apparent want was actually a need.

Once you've gone through the entire list all you have to do is put the needs into the search parameters of your multiple listing service. It will then pull up only those properties that meet your clients' needs. Then you can rank them by how many of the wants they also offer.

You can do the same process with sellers to rank offers that may be submitted. Make the same chart and list everything they want in the perfect offer on the left-hand side of the paper, including price, terms, condition, closing length, and anything else they want. Then ask, "If you received an offer that was otherwise perfect, but it didn't have this item, would you still consider it?" By determining their needs, you know what the perfect offer would look like and how important various contract items are to them. This process will save you, your seller, other agents, and potential buyers a great deal of time and grief.

If you take the time to separate needs from wants for both your buyers and sellers, everyone, including you, will benefit.

32) PROVIDE SELLERS WITH QUESTIONS THEY CAN ASK AGENTS

Most sellers want to interview at least three agents before listing their house. The problem is that they don't have a clue what questions to ask. If this is the case, why not give them a list of questions they can ask all the agents so they can compare "apples with apples." This helps you because you can contour the list to highlight your own strengths and minimize your weaknesses, as well as showcase your experience and background. It's a great marketing tool, but it looks like you're just helping the client screen for the best agent.

For instance, the first question I have sellers ask other agents is "Are you a Certified Residential Specialist?" Since very few agents have earned this designation, when my name shows up as the only CRS, I look like I'm in an elite group. Obviously, if you are not a CRS you shouldn't use this question, but perhaps you have earned another designation. If so, you would start by asking if all the agents have earned this or any other designation that works in your favor. If you haven't earned any designations, it's time to do so.

Another question I suggest sellers ask agents is "How many listings do you currently have?" At first glance, it would appear that a lower number would work against you. I, for one, don't take a lot of listings because, as a professional real estate speaker and trainer, I'm on the road over a hundred days a year. I sell this as a benefit to clients by letting them know that they aren't going to be crowded out by other clients. Being on a short list means that I'll have more time to devote to them. I cap it off with the idea that I'm very particular about the listings I take. "Be sure," I tell them, "that your agent has the time to personally market your house. Shouldn't it receive the attention it deserves?"

Another question sellers might want to ask has to do with marketing, which is crucial to getting a listing sold. So I have sellers ask prospective agents, "How will you market my property?" Most agents only do the minimum—they just put listings in the local newspaper and the REALTORS® Multiple Listing Service, then close their eyes and hope it sells. Sellers need to be told that there are only a handful of really serious buyers for any property. To maximize price and minimize time, they have to target their marketing to reach the people who are most likely to buy. The whole point in asking the simple question, "How will you market my property?" is to illustrate that you know all about this. Do the other agents?

Offer a list of questions sellers can ask agents and they will love you for it. However, recognize that unprepared agents will not feel quite so appreciative.

33) DEVELOP A LIST OF QUESTIONS THAT BUYERS CAN ASK AGENTS

Buyers, especially first timers, don't know how to select an agent to help them buy the home of their dreams. It should be like a job interview where the most qualified candidate gets the job, but most buyers just start working with an agent until they discover they don't like him or he's incompetent, and then they start looking for another.

Why not save clients all of this heartache and headache? Consider developing a list of interview questions that buyers can use to select an agent.

The questions on your list might include the following:

- What do you know about financing a home and how did you learn it?
- How do I know which is the best loan for my situation?
- How would you increase the chances of my offer getting accepted in a multiple offer situation?
- How will you efficiently help me find the home of my dreams?
- Do you use a Buyer-Broker Agreement?
- Why should I sign a Buyer-Broker Agreement with you?
- What is your experience in negotiating?
- What real estate designations do you hold?

You can attract buyers to your website by offering a free list of questions that all buyers should ask prospective agents. Having this list will separate you from your competition. It is very similar to the list you would use for sellers and works to your advantage in similar ways. It makes you look like the good guy. Again, there is nothing wrong in designing the list to highlight your strengths and the weaknesses of your competition.

34) BE A CONSULTANT—NOT A SALESPERSON

What's the difference between a salesperson and a consultant? Besides the fact that people generally dislike salespeople and respect consultants, salespeople will do anything to make the sale while consultants will tell you both the positives and the negatives, so you know what you're getting. Consultants are experts who provide impartial advice to clients. For salespeople, the transaction is geared, first and foremost, toward their own interests—making the sale. Salespeople are generally thought of by the public as self-interested purveyors of products or services, so their recommendations are sometimes suspect. The public expects them to say whatever makes them or their product look good, whether it's true or not.

You want to be able to tell people the truth without worrying about losing them as clients just because you convey something they don't want to hear. In order to be a real estate consultant, you must have a steady stream of clients so you aren't in the unenviable position of having to accept everyone who walks in the door.

Train yourself to look at every transaction from the perspective of both sellers and buyers, no matter who you actually represent. As a consultant, you would inform sellers about what they need to know, and even share the less pleasant facts of life, including the following:

- Pricing
- Marketing
- Staging
- Depreciation issues such as small rooms, lack of a dining room, lack of garage, older appliances, deferred maintenance
- External factors such as schools, freeways, apartment houses, gas stations, and the like, that are too close to a house and can affect its value
- Outside factors such as mortgage interest rates, income tax developments, and the economy that can affect their property value

You would tell your buyers what they need to know about these issues:

- Inspections they should order and pay for
- Depreciation issues such as small rooms, lack of a dining room, lack of a garage, older appliances, deferred maintenance, and so on
- External factors such as schools, freeways, apartment houses, gas stations and the like, that might be so close to the house that they would affect its value
- Outside factors such as mortgage interest rates, income tax developments, and the state of the economy

Expired listing clients would have to be consulted about the following:

- How hard it is to sell a property that everyone thinks they've seen
- What it takes to make an expired listing attractive again
- What price it will take to get the property sold now
- Staging and other factors that can make a house seem new and exciting on the market

Owners who are trying to sell their own houses would need to know about these topics:

- What it really takes to sell a house
- How having a limited number of buyers adversely affects sales price
- What kind of buyers are attracted to FSBOs
- That only 14 percent of FSBOs a year sell without an agent

Telling clients about all these points educates them so they can make an informed choice. This stands in stark contrast to a salesperson, who would not take the time to tell them a thing unless it directly leads to a sale.

35) NEVER QUOTE YOUR COMMISSION UNTIL YOU ESTABLISH VALUE

Many potential sellers today want agents to tell them how much commission they will charge before they even begin their listing presentation. It is as if they want to eliminate you right away if the figure is too high. My recommendation is not to quote a fee until you have had a chance to determine the needs of the seller.

How would you feel if a doctor started quoting a cost for treatment before he had examined you? In fact, this is the exact analogy I use with clients. The fact is that all agents aren't the same and neither are clients. We have to treat each person as if she is a unique case. You can't approach a real estate transaction with a cookie-cutter mentality. The first thing you need to do is determine what the client's individual problem is because your primary task is to solve it. The task itself is what determines how much work, expertise, and skill will be required, and you can't quote your commission until that is established.

For example, if I know that a client is engaging in a tax-deferred exchange or getting a divorce, I will usually charge more for that transaction than I would for one that requires fewer challenges. But if I'm talking to a seller about a listing and it is a sellers' market, I might charge at the lower end of my commission range because it shouldn't take very long to sell. My only stipulation is that he must be willing to do everything I suggest to market the property. On the other hand, if I'm selling a house in a buyers' market and I'm going to have to spend a lot of time and money to get it sold, shouldn't I charge a higher fee to cover my costs?

When determining the commission rate for a buyer in a Buyer-Broker Agreement, again it depends on the facts and circumstances. If the client is looking for a standard house in a buyers' market, that would probably dictate a fee at the lower end of the spectrum. However, if she is selling a unique property at a time when sellers are not regularly receiving multiple offers, that would dictate a higher commission. I am going to have to expend much more time, effort, and possibly money to meet her needs.

For sellers and buyers, use some of the techniques above to establish your value, analyze the client's situation, look at the property (sellers only), and review current market conditions. After all that, quote your commission.

If a seller demands that you quote a fee before you can analyze his situation, walk away—he is obviously not interested in value.

36) KNOW HOW TO QUOTE YOUR COMPENSATION

Properly quoting your compensation is almost always a botched job. Both sellers and buyers believe that real estate professionals make a fortune because we always quote the commission for the entire transaction. Stop it!

The problem with the way we discuss our fee is that we tell clients the total fee for the listing and the selling agent. The fact is—we don't get that. The listing agent only gets the listing fee, which is generally three percent maximum. The selling agent gets the other portion, which is usually the same.

Everyone in the business knows it is a split fee, but we don't tell the public that. Can you blame people for thinking an agent charges too much when we always quote the fee for the work of both the listing and selling agents? That's like saying that a lawyer who hires a financial planner for a client gets $400 an hour, when in fact, he gets $200 an hour and the planner gets the other $200.

Another scenario occurs when you are talking to a prospective seller, trying to get her to sign with you. The first thing she says is, "Why should I pay you seven percent when I know a guy who charges six percent commission?" I explain that for the one-percent difference, this is what I have to offer. Right away, I have changed the numbers on the playing field. I am no longer trying to defend seven percent; I only have to justify that tiny one percent, which is a lot easier to explain away. Illustrate for the client, in terms she cannot fail to see, how much more work you are willing to do for only one percent. In other words, sell the value of this tiny difference she will be paying.

The reason we get less resistance when asking buyers to sign a Buyer-Broker Agreement is that we are generally only focusing on the selling agent's compensation. Shouldn't we be doing the same for the listing commission?

37) USE THE Realtor® CODE OF ETHICS TO SELL YOUR VALUE

In over 30 years in the real estate profession, I am not aware of any member of the National Association of Realtors® who brings the Code of Ethics to a meeting with a potential seller, buyer, expired listing, or for-sale-by-owner. Yet, it is one of the most powerful ways to sell your value to clients, because the public has high ethical expectations when it comes to the biggest transaction most of them will ever conduct. However, few are even aware that we live by a code of ethics. We must educate our clients that the REALTORS® Code protects them during a time when they are putting their financial future in our hands. They will be reassured to find out that there are official safeguards. By sharing the Code with them, it implies that you are high minded enough to be concerned about fair play and want your client to know it. That's why I would hand a copy of it to every client. Whether or not they actually read it is immaterial; just giving it to them speaks volumes about your stand on ethics. The Code of Ethics holds us to incredibly high standards of practice and care. Giving them a copy says that we are not salespeople but real estate professionals.

Be sure to mention the purpose of the major sections. The Preamble to the Code pretty much says it all: "The term REALTOR® has come to connote competency, fairness, and high integrity resulting from adherence to a lofty ideal of moral conduct in business relations. No inducement of profit and no instruction from clients ever can justify departure from this ideal."

Just the first section, "Duties to Clients and Customers," requires members to protect and promote the interest of our clients. It prohibits us from misleading owners about the market value of their properties and requires us to preserve the confidentiality of information we receive. It says that we will not misrepresent pertinent facts relating to the property, we will cooperate with other brokers, and that contracts will be clear and understandable. This also implies that our information, including that on our website, should be current and accurate. This section alone gives us plenty of ethical responsibilities. But wait, there's more.

The second section, "Duties to the Public," says we will provide our services without discrimination and that we will provide competent services in all aspects of our work. It also requires us to be honest in advertising and cooperate with any investigation of our practices.

The third section, "Duties to REALTORS®," says that we will respect our competitors and not interfere with their relationships with their clients, and we will arbitrate any disputes between REALTORS®.

The Code of Ethics holds us to incredibly high standards of practice and care. It should give our clients confidence when we are handling the biggest transaction of their lives.

38) RESPOND TO CALLS AND EMAILS PROMPTLY

Nothing says that you value a client's time and his business like returning telephone calls promptly. It not only communicates that you are professional, but gives the client a sense of security as well. Remember that first-time home buyers and sellers are especially afraid and uneasy about the transaction. Treating them like they're important helps reassure them that they are not alone in this transaction.

This is not to say that you must interrupt everything you are doing to return calls immediately. *Promptly* means within a few hours and many agents leave a voice-mail message letting people know that they return phone calls between certain times which they have set aside solely for this purpose.

You should respond to emails in a timely manner as well. In fact, people expect emails to be returned within a couple of hours or they will quickly do business with someone else. Make it a habit to check your email in the morning, at lunch, and at the end of the day. People who email you after business hours generally don't expect to receive a response until the next morning. If their communication were urgent, they'd pick up the good old telephone and call you.

Failing to return phone calls and emails in a timely manner causes clients to imagine the worst possible scenarios: perhaps you've been in an accident or maybe you don't want to talk to them because you've given up on them as clients. After the feeling of dread has passed, clients just become angry because they feel they are being ignored. Ignoring someone is the worst possible punishment one can inflict on another human being. Most people would prefer corporal punishment or even downright torture to the pain of being ignored. Before we had laws to punish wrongdoers, people who committed crimes against society were simply shunned or ignored. These were thought to be the worst forms of punishment possible. So don't punish your clients. Be professional and return all communications promptly.

I have only one exception to this rule. If someone leaves me an angry telephone message or sends me a negative email, I will wait 24 hours before responding so that my own negative response has a chance to subside. I send an email saying I have received their note and will respond within 24 hours so I don't throw more fuel onto the flame and make them think I'm ignoring them yet again. For telephone messages, I leave a similar message at a time when I know they will not be in to receive the call, like during lunch or before work.

39) PROVIDE A LIST OF SERVICE PROVIDERS

Another way to sell your value to clients is to develop a list of service providers that they can rely on. Make sure these professionals are reliable by listening carefully to your clients' feedback. If you hear of problems, contact the service provider and determine what went wrong. If the complaints continue, it's time to find another vendor.

Start your list by getting recommendations of service providers from your past clients or fellow agents. You are not necessarily looking for the least expensive company in the area, but obviously you want someone who is, at a minimum, reliable, efficient, responsive, friendly, and patient.

Just some of the types of service providers to consider adding to your list include the following:

- Gardeners
- Carpet cleaners
- Carpenters
- Chimney cleaners
- Electricians
- Roofers

- Contractors
- Landscapers
- Pool cleaners
- Plumbers
- Handypersons
- Haulers
- Movers
- Accountants
- Attorneys
- Financial planners
- Stereo and television installers
- Computer repair persons
- Auto repair persons

I know agents who make a bound reference book and even charge vendors an annual advertising fee to be featured in the book. Each gets to put a description of his services and may even include a discount. The agent then distributes the book to all of her clients. This book is another tangible demonstration of an agent's value.

Other agents make their lists available online through their websites. This way there can be a feedback mechanism about each of the vendors so clients can rate their experiences. Obviously, if one of the providers consistently receives low marks or complaints, you would not invite them to participate the next year.

This question always comes up: "What is my liability if one of the vendors doesn't do a good job or is unscrupulous in some way?" I believe the answer is the same as it would be for a newspaper running an ad for a local auto mechanic who is sued by his customers—none. You're just an advertising medium. Customers always have to exercise their own due diligence before spending money. However, you should check with your own attorney about the liability laws in the jurisdiction in which you practice.

40) DEVELOP A BUYERS' KIT

Another way to visibly demonstrate your value to home buyers is to give them a kit with everything they need to be an active part of the home buying process. If a buyer wants to work with me and signs a Buyer-Broker Agreement, I give her a large canvas bag containing the following items:

- Local map
- Notepad
- Pens and pencils
- Highlighter
- Pad of sticky notes
- Pad of sticky arrows. These allow my buyer to "point" to where various properties are on a map so she can easily refer to them later.
- Plastic raincoat (during the winter) for visiting open homes
- Stack of my business cards in case she wants to look at open houses without me
- Bottle of aspirin. I explain that looking for just the right home is going to be a lot of work and could cause a few headaches.
- Website address (www.efax.com) that enables her to receive faxes on her computer. As you know, a lot of paperwork needs to be sent to the buyer.

Not only does the Buyers' Kit add value and differentiate you from your competition, but it clearly indicates to clients how much work it is to help them buy a home, which is why you need to be appropriately compensated.

Consider putting your name and contact information prominently on the bag. This way you get free advertising every time the buyer is out looking at properties. My clients show it to their friends and ask if their agent provides the same "goody bag" (they don't).

41) LEARN HOW TO COMMUNICATE WITH MULTICULTURAL CLIENTS

Hispanics, African Americans, Asians, Middle Easterners, and others are a fast-growing home buyer market. According to the National Association of REALTORS®, 60 percent of all home buyers today are minorities. This can be a lucrative market for agents and brokers who know how to meet these buyers' unique needs. You would do well to learn the cultural differences and adjust your practices if you want to attract and retain this section of the market.

Just a few of the cultural differences to be aware of include the following:

- Meeting and greeting: Many people from diverse cultures are not comfortable with shaking hands. In fact, it can be very offensive if their cultural and/or religious beliefs discourage it. Instead of assuming, let the customers determine how they should be greeted.
- Personal space: In the United States, people usually stand about 2.5 feet apart when conversing. Recognize that people from certain cultures usually stand closer or farther apart when talking. Again, let the customer determine the personal space that works for him.
- Eye contact: In America, direct eye contact while conversing is considered respectful and a sign of honesty. However, in other parts of the world it is considered rude and disrespectful to look someone in the eye, so people avert their eyes in a conversation. Just accept this as a sign of respect, even though it goes against what you're used to.
- Contracts: In the United States, we put everything we agree upon in writing, while elsewhere they are less formal. Also, here, signing the contract ends all negotiations, while in other cultures it may just begin the bargaining process.

- Beliefs: In this country, we have various beliefs about bad luck—not letting black cats cross our paths, not walking under ladders, and avoiding the number 13. Other cultures have their own beliefs about where they live and whether the house faces an auspicious direction or has a lucky address. Learning something about feng shui principles could be helpful in dealing with some Asian home buyers.
- Inquiry: It's okay to ask people about their culture because they want you to understand them as a people. However, make it a practice to ask EVERYONE, not just those who may look different from mainstream Americans.

To learn more about understanding how cultural differences can affect real estate transactions, see my book *OPENING DOORS: Selling to Multicultural Real Estate Clients* (Oakhill Press, 1999).

42) REDUCE YOUR CLIENTS' LIABILITY

It's crucial to educate all of your clients about the liabilities involved in buying or selling a property. Sellers, for instance, must properly disclose the condition of their properties. Buyers must make sure the house they're buying is sound or they could have liability in the future when they go to sell.

Through your training and experience, you can reduce your sellers' and buyers' liability. The real estate business is fraught with peril, and lawsuits abound because so much can go wrong. You are sometimes the only buffer between your client and a lawsuit. Your job is to make sure all disclosures required by law and good business practice are provided to the buyer. Even when these might hurt the salability of the property, it's better to disclose than not to. Sooner or later, these issues will surface.

You and your seller must disclose any red flags that could be a cause for concern, and any material facts that could affect the buyer's decision to purchase the property. They might not seem important, but it's best to be thorough. I have a rule that if these words ever cross my mind—"I wonder if I should disclose this..."—disclose it! If there is a dispute down the line, an attorney will ask you if it occurred to you to disclose this point. He'll tell you that you should have.

You reduce your seller's liability by checking on any questions about the square footage of a building or the amount of land that is being sold. When in doubt, check it out. Have your seller pay for a survey if necessary to verify these representations.

You reduce your buyers' liability by making sure that they meet all contractual deadlines and perform as promised. Failing to do so could not only create liability for them, but cause them to lose the property to another buyer.

You also want to be sure you know the form of the down payment. In the old days, say 10 years ago, it wasn't uncommon for buyers to give their agents a check to hold onto for the deposit, even when they didn't exactly have the funds to back it up. This was not usually a problem though. If the purchase agreement was ratified, the buyer would quickly make a deposit to cover the check.

Unfortunately, a number of lawsuits around the country have made this practice *illegal,* unless the agent for the buyer first discloses that there are insufficient funds to cover the check. What the buyer is trying to do here is lock up the property to keep others from bidding on it. In the most honest scenario, he always intended to back the check as soon as he could transfer the funds from another account. But ultimately he changed his mind about buying the property and then the deal fell through. In the worst scenario, the person never intended for the check to go through; he was just trying to hold onto the property for someone else. He never does put the money in the bank, and then he defaults on the sale. Unfortunately for the seller, there is no money to claim as damages, and all the other interested parties are gone. The house has to go back on the market.

The agent representing the buyer cannot get off the hook very easily in this scenario. She can be sued for lack of disclosure, breach of fiduciary duties, misrepresentation, and more.

In addition to being solvent enough to cover any checks they write, your buyers should also obtain all appropriate inspections of the property they're interested in. Inform them that they can have pest control, roof, contractor, well water, septic, soil, and many other inspections conducted, depending on the area they live in. If these inspections are not properly conducted, the value of the property they're buying might end up being a lot lower than they believe, and this will give rise to liability later on when they're ready to sell.

43) SAVE YOUR CLIENTS TIME

In America, you often hear the phrase "time is money." Saving time is seen as more important even than saving money because you can always get more money; you cannot ever get more time. When it's gone, it's gone. It is the one truly nonrenewable resource. So if you can show your sellers that you can save them time, then money will not be as much of a concern to them.

So how can you save your sellers time? Think about all the tasks you are trained to do that they would have to do themselves if they were to sell their house on their own. This illustrates, more than anything, how time-valuable you are to them and why you are well worth your commission. The public has absolutely no idea how much time you're saving them until you tell them, and once you have, they're always impressed.

Here are just a few examples of how you save your sellers time. You do the following:

- Obtain a preliminary title report that shows who owns the property, what liens are against it, and more

- Provide a "For Sale" sign. Otherwise they would have to buy one at the local hardware store and find a way to make it visible in their front yard
- Take pictures of the property and make flyers for it
- Write a description for the multiple listing service
- Place the property into the multiple listing service
- Develop a targeted marketing plan
- Put the property on the Internet, such as at www.realtor.com or your company's website
- Hold the house open for buyers to see
- Meet potential buyers at the property at times other than open house day
- Take phone calls and answer questions about the property from other agents
- Receive offers from potential buyers
- Make sure that escrow has been opened
- Arrange for inspections

You save a lot of time for buyers as well, and this provides a tremendous service to them. Time is very precious today and people will pay a lot of money to save it. Just look at all the time-saving appliances like dishwashers and microwave ovens that people buy all the time. Buying a new home is an all-consuming activity that can be a black hole, sucking in all of a person's free time—unless she has an agent who knows what he's doing.

Here are some of the ways we save buyers time. We do the following:

- Research the market for properties that meet their specific needs
- Contact owners and agents to make sure that properties are still for sale
- Arrange for showings of the properties to clients
- Determine the most efficient route to show properties so buyers aren't driving in circles looking for the address

- Write offers that reflect the buyer's needs
- Present offers to sellers and their agents
- Arrange for inspections of ratified properties
- Protect the buyer's interests at all times. This is important because when a person has someone looking out for him, he knows there won't be any surprises that come up after he thinks the deal is sealed. He knows his agent is on top of it.

If you save your clients time they will reward you well because, after all, time is money.

44) HELP CHILDREN COPE WITH A MOVE

Whether moving to or from a house, most adults tend to under-estimate how traumatic it is for children. Even for adults it's hard; it is one of the top 10 factors that cause stress in our lives. Could it be less difficult for children, who don't even have the semblance of control? Involving parents in helping their children transition from one location to another is crucial. I have seen transactions fall apart because the children literally were too traumatized by the move.

As a real estate agent, you can play a part. Make sure your clients are keeping their kids informed about what is going on because it might not occur to them to do so. You have been through this hundreds if not thousands of times, so you know more than they do about how hard this can be for young ones. Children largely operate on intuition, so they actually know much more than you think because they quietly observe everything around them. Waiting until the day of the move can be a disaster! That's when there's too much going on and everyone's nerves are on edge. Kids have probably already formulated their fears and this is the day you have designated to deal with them. Ask the parents to explain the move as soon as possible, before the angst and anxiety grows.

To play a part in this, have the parents introduce you. Talk to them a little about how they feel about the move and then explain your role. Involve the child in the move as much as you can.

When there are small children involved, get them to visualize themselves in the new house in general, and their room specifically. When working with sellers with small children, who are leaving possibly the only home they've ever known, you have to get them excited about where they are going and minimize the emotional attachments to the house they are leaving.

Many real estate agents tend to downplay the importance of moving from an apartment to a home since the buyers are just upgrading their lifestyle. However, children don't recognize the difference between renting and owning. All they know is that their apartment is a home—a familiar and safe place—and you are uprooting them from it. Agents can look like the bad guys and become hated by children, who will then do everything they can to sabotage the move. If you take the time to explain why the move is necessary and how it benefits them, you can win them over before it turns into a problem. We already discussed pulling homeowners away from the emotions that tie them to the property they're in; we must do the same for children.

Remind the parents to try to be as positive about the move as possible. If they have any worries or points of contention, they should discuss it out of hearing distance of the kids. Talk about the whole thing as an adventure, and ask the children to come up with ideas about how they can help with it. They should not be left on the sidelines during the move, but given specific duties they select themselves. These could be nothing more than "make-believe" chores, as long as they accomplish the goal—keep the kids occupied and don't give them time to fixate on their fears that they'll never make another friend as long as they live.

Suggest that parents watch for warning signs that children are not adjusting well to the move. Some signs include anxiety, depression, significant disruptions in sleep, fighting with their siblings or friends, and falling grades in school. Some children even need professional mental health services to help them adjust to their new environment. If so, seek help early.

45) BUILD VALUE BY BEING CONSISTENT

Relationships are built on reliability. If your clients know they can consistently rely on you, they'll use you over and over because it's a lot better than taking a chance with somebody new. Also, clients who rely on you will pay more than an average fee just because it's worth it to them.

Look at your own life. You probably don't go to the cheapest mechanic, hairdresser, dry cleaner, or tailor. You could, but then you would have to put up with sloppier service. People pay top dollar to have work done right the first time and every time so they don't have to worry about it—and so will your clients.

Clients also expect consistency with a real estate professional. We all want that with a product or service. When you turn on the ignition in your car, you want it to start every time or it disrupts your life. My very first new car was a beautiful Alfa Romeo sports car, which I loved. However, whenever I was running late for an appointment with a client, it had a terrible habit of not starting. I always had to make all sorts of apologies to my clients, then go without transportation while it was towed to the repair shop. And then the mechanics never found anything wrong with it. As much as I loved that car, eventually I had to trade it in for something more reliable. That's how important consistency is—it's more important than love.

Inconsistencies can make clients very uncomfortable, not to mention confused. Where are you? Why haven't you delivered the papers to be signed? Why didn't you make the offer on time? They aren't paying you to fail, they're paying you to do what has to be done in a timely way. Sometimes the inconsistency is between what they expected and what they got. When that happens, they will immediately start looking for another agent because that is a recipe for disappointment.

Here are some ways to demonstrate your reliability and consistency to clients:

- Do what you say you're going to do so they know they can count on you.
- Be honest. If you don't know the answer to a question just say so. People who bluff sound more ignorant than people who just don't have the answer at that moment.
- Under-promise and over-deliver. This is always a pleasant surprise.
- Tell them both the positives and negatives about every property so they know you're not just painting a pretty picture to talk them into buying.
- Be organized because it tells them that you're on top of things and you think they're important.
- Be just as concerned and caring about clients after close of escrow as you were during the transaction; otherwise, they will believe you were just after their money.
- Obey all traffic laws whenever you are driving with clients in the car. How would they feel if you blew through a red light just as you were lecturing them about the real estate Code of Ethics?

Look for other areas in your business where you can practice consistency and reliability. If you do, clients will really appreciate it.

46) BECOME A REAL ESTATE RESOURCE

You can increase your value to clients by becoming their resource for anything related to real estate, not just the buying or selling of property. In other words, any time they think of something related to our business—such as finding an apartment for their college-age child, buying a time-share, investing in a real estate partnership, or buying investment property—they should be able to call you first.

This is not to say that you have to become the expert in everything real estate related, but it does mean you should know who to refer clients to whenever an issue arises. When people think of real estate, your name should pop up. Just keep prompting your clients that whenever they have a question that is even slightly real estate related, they should call you first.

You might even periodically send them a reminder that you can help them with some of the following issues:

- Buying a modular home
- Buying a mobile home
- Buying a time-share
- Buying a vacation home
- Buying investment property
- Buying a recreational vehicle
- Selling a recreational vehicle
- Renting an apartment
- Buying real estate through an auction
- Building their dream house
- Investing in commercial real estate
- Renting corporate housing
- Buying foreclosure property
- Buying a home in a golf community
- Buying home insurance
- Buying international real estate
- Buying or selling a farm
- Buying or selling a ranch

47) USE PAPERWORK TO DEMONSTRATE YOUR VALUE

We real estate professionals are always complaining about the huge amount of paperwork required to close a real estate transaction. However, this can be a benefit when trying to visibly show clients how much work is involved.

If you show your clients the thickness of a closed transaction folder from another buyer, it will visibly demonstrate exactly how much paperwork is involved in this monumental purchase. My closed files, on average, are about two inches thick, and potential buyers are always amazed at how much work is required to help them acquire the home of their dreams. Sellers are equally befuddled by the volume of documentation required just for them to sell their house. From contracts to disclosures, financing, inspections, title, escrow, and more, it's amazing to us as well as our clients how much work we must do to earn our money.

When choosing the file to show your clients, be sure to protect the privacy of the person whose file you have pulled. Remember, the point is only to show the thickness, not go through it in detail.

To select the thickest file you may want to look for transactions that include the following:

- Financing for the purchase of a home
- Condominium or town-house with covenants, conditions, and restrictions
- Additional disclosures
- Extra inspections such as septic tanks or wells
- Easements or restrictions
- Extensive repair work required
- Seller carryback financing
- Other unusual aspects

Remind every client that paperwork is only one small part of the process of buying or selling a home.

MARKETING

48) GATHER WRITTEN TESTIMONIALS FROM SATISFIED CLIENTS

One of the biggest challenges in selling our value to clients is the fact that real estate services are intangible and most certainly difficult to describe. No one can know how good we really are until they try us. Unfortunately, the newspapers are full of horror stories from sellers or buyers who ended up with the agent from hell.

Testimonial letters are an effective tool for broadcasting our accomplishments and talents; they're better than anything we can say about ourselves. People who have done business with us in the past can "sell us" in ways we cannot do ourselves, because they can explain what we have to offer so that it doesn't sound like bragging. In fact, you can even suggest to potential clients that they call former clients just to verify that what was said in the letter is true. You may be surprised to find that past clients will downright embarrass you with their words of praise.

Whenever you hand a check to a seller or the house keys to a buyer, ask them to sit down right then and there to write you a testimonial letter. That is the moment of greatest satisfaction, when you are held in the highest regard. If you wait, they're more likely to forget or become too busy. When you ask for a letter right at close of escrow, you are counting on their enthusiasm to be at its strongest.

To make it easier for them to do this, bring notepaper and a high-quality pen with you. I find that quick-drying gel pens work the best because you want to fold the letter immediately and tuck it in your briefcase.

Here's a template that you can ask your clients to follow. You're not telling them what to write—if they want to compose their own letter, you would certainly let them. This just makes it easier: "I used (agent's name) in the sale/purchase of my house/home at (address). During this transaction, I found (agent's first name) to be . . . and he/she helped me by (specific examples)."

Some points to remind your clients to cover, depending on the nature of the transaction, might include the following:

- Professionalism
- Breadth of knowledge
- Familiarity with the area
- Reliability
- Interest in the client's needs
- Enthusiasm
- Negotiation skills

You can also ask them to elaborate on how you overcame any challenges or solved any problems that came up during the transaction.

If you don't get your testimonial letters on the spot, you're going to have to be persistent because people often have good intentions at first, but they do get busy and distracted, or they just forget. You have to ask several times before you actually receive your letter. Sometimes the client is perfectly willing to sign his name, but he just doesn't want to go through the trouble of writing it himself and that's okay.

Just write the letter yourself and let him sign it. Make sure you tune in to the specifics of how you helped this individual and include him in the letter. Don't say anything the client might object to. He has to feel comfortable with it if he is going to sign his name.

Another way to help a client compose an effective testimonial letter is to show her several samples that you are proud of. Usually after seeing how others have structured their letters, this client will be more than capable of customizing her own.

The most effective time to use your testimonial letters with a potential client is just as you are getting ready to ask him to sign a listing contract or Buyer-Broker Agreement. If the person was having any hesitancy at all about working with you, the letter should eliminate it.

49) GATHER VIDEO TESTIMONIALS FROM SATISFIED CLIENTS

While written testimonial letters are very effective in selling your value, video testimonials are even better because potential clients can actually see and hear past clients saying how great you are. Videos tend to be much more vivid, compelling, and believable than letters, which, after all, are somewhat anonymous. You can't see or hear the author. But for clients to be filmed means they are really committed to what they are saying about you.

The power of a visual testimonial cannot be overestimated because it reaches your clients at a deep emotional level. In addition, it would be rare for your competitors to have a video. The fact that you alone have one implies that you do a better job.

Not only are video testimonials more credible than written testimonials, but they are often easier to obtain. People always have a lot more resistance to writing than to speaking, which they just find easier. And it saves you work because you don't have to write the letter for them and then get them to sign it. With video, all you have to do is set up a small digital camera on a tripod, stand behind it, and press record. Then just ask your clients to look directly at you as if the camera weren't there, and talk about how they felt the transaction went. They will absolutely embarrass you with their praise.

Once you have the person on video, you can ask a techie or a local teenager to help you edit the clip. All you do next is download the digital file to your computer and insert it in the testimonial section of your listing presentation. There are many parts to your sales pitch, and all but this one are set in stone. They're pretty much the same for everyone. This testimonial section, however, will be customized for each individual potential client you approach. Once you sit down, you talk to him for a while and establish a rapport. This is a back-and-forth process where you both ask and answer questions. Then you begin your formal seller or buyer listing presentation. Some agents have a binder of printed material that they flip through, and then augment the visual with a verbal explanation.

Nowadays, many of us are more high-tech. Once I have established a comfortable atmosphere with a one-on-one conversation, the rest of my presentation is all on the laptop computer. Toward the end of it, to seal the deal, up comes the testimonial. As I said, this is customized for the individual client watching it. What this means is that I group my clips by the type and price of property so I know what to select for a particular presentation. They might be condominiums, starter homes, medium-priced properties, or upscale houses. If, for example, you are a condominium buyer, you will only want to hear testimonials from purchasers of that type of property. You don't care about upscale homes on golf courses. If the prospective client is a condominium seller, she will be interested in how you might sell the benefits of restrictive covenants, conditions, and restrictions (CC&Rs). The testimonial will sell the idea that you know how to negotiate on this point and that you explained the CC&Rs in a way that made them understandable and acceptable. Higher-end owners might talk about how creative you were in marketing to high-end buyers and that you helped protect their privacy by screening out looky-loos and others who weren't serious.

Each of my video clips of testimonials lasts no longer than 90 seconds because any more than that seems over the top. Since I place three of them back-to-back, altogether, the testimonial lasts about five minutes.

I find that it is best to show this part just before I ask my clients to sign a contract. It really seems to overcome any last bits of resistance when they see and hear people who have been genuinely satisfied with my services. Timing is crucial because when the "movie" is over, you just need to hand the clients a pen and show them where to sign. If you don't capitalize on this moment, you'll lose the momentum the videos have created.

50) SEND NEWSLETTERS ON A REGULAR BASIS... FOR FREE

Nothing builds value faster in the minds of clients than providing valuable information on a regular basis. The newsletter is a good vehicle because it has more staying power than emails if it is attractive, professional, and well written. It often sits on the coffee table where people can hand it to their friends. But for it to work, it has to contain relevant information. Make sure you send it out at least once a quarter because if you don't stay in regular touch with your clients, someone else will. As a bonus to its value, the same newsletter you send to current clients can also be used to regularly market to area homes you want to reach on a regular basis.

Yes, email newsletters can be sent for next to nothing, but with all the spam filters these days it's hard to get through, and people don't often read them. This is why so many savvy agents have gone back to printed newsletters. However, agents don't send printed newsletters out as often as they should because they can be expensive to print and mail. But, would you do it if it cost you nothing?

How do you send printed newsletters for free? Do what newspapers do—sell advertising space. Ask yourself, "Who would be interested in getting their name out in my area?" Well, anyone who makes a living off home owners. The following are just a few examples:

- Carpenters
- Electricians
- Plumbers
- Carpet cleaners
- Landscapers
- Painters
- Home repair people
- Title companies
- Lenders
- Attorneys
- Accountants
- Financial planners
- Retail stores

I can hear all your objections now: "But I don't want to cold-call all these vendors. I'm already busy enough. And by the way, I don't want to sit down and write this thing every few months. This all sounds like a lot of work and one more claim on my time!"

To answer these objections, we have to circle back to advertising, which pretty much covers everything. You can hire a college student to round up advertisers for you, and you can hire a freelance writer (they're everywhere) to write the copy for you. One alteration to the latter point is that you can also purchase a prewritten real estate newsletter, which you can then customize and use articles from according to what is pertinent to your area.

To ensure that all your costs are completely covered, you first compute the total cost of having someone write your newsletter, the price of printing, postage, folding (if necessary), and anything else associated with it. I even hired a college marketing student to find my advertisers and added his salary plus commission into these costs.

Next, divide that cost by the number of ads you can reasonably fit in. Don't have so many ads that they overwhelm the content. After all, you do want clients to read your articles, so ads should not total more than one-quarter of each page. You simply need to charge advertisers enough to cover the cost of your newsletter.

As long as the cost of the ad is less than what it would cost advertisers to send out a flyer on their own, they will probably sign up. They might even pay more because an agent who has been regularly sending a newsletter for several years has far more credibility than someone sending a flyer for the first time.

51) CLEARLY TARGET YOUR MARKETING TO BUYERS

If your marketing is not clearly targeted to attract the most likely buyers for your listings, you are wasting a lot of peoples' time, energy, and gas. Buyers are only interested in homes that meet their needs and that they can afford.

A particular property will attract a certain type of buyer and no others. If you want to attract that person, develop a *buyer profile*. Sit down and answer the following:

- How old would the person be?
- Should he be working class, middle class, or upper class?
- Would she have any children? How many?
- What does she do for fun?
- What radio stations would he listen to?
- What newspapers and magazines would he read?
- What television programs would she watch?

Knowing the answers to these questions will help you reach buyers in the most effective ways. For instance, if I have a high-end luxury home for sale, I'm not going to advertise in the local newspaper because, in my area, the average income of the person reading our paper is just $60,000 per year. The average reader could never afford a $2 million property. Instead, I'll advertise in newsletters published for members of local golf clubs, the horse riding academy, boating clubs, ski clubs, and the like. These are much less expensive yet more effective media outlets for reaching upscale buyers than the local newspaper. It is surprising that few agents in my area even think of such a targeted marketing program.

To increase the effectiveness of your marketing, consider attending a free ad writing class. Where can you get such a class? Simple. Every newspaper in America would be happy to give you a class on how to write more effective ads using headlines, engaging words, calls to action, and more. Why would a newspaper provide you with such a service? They know that if your ads are more effective, you will run more of them. It's quite self-serving, but makes perfect sense, so why not take advantage of the service?

All you have to do is contact the advertising manager at your local newspaper and tell them what you need. Frankly, they will probably be dumbfounded, but they'll also be flattered because very few real estate professionals ever contact them to learn about advertising.

52) SELL BENEFITS, NOT FEATURES

Clients only care about the benefit of what you can do for them. Unfortunately, most of the time agents talk about *features* rather than *benefits*. What's the difference? A personal feature is the knowledge or experience an agent has gained, like a master's degree or 100 closed transactions. A property feature is a specific characteristic of a house, such as a deck or fireplace. A benefit, on the other hand, is what any of these do for the client. A master's degree in finance provides knowledge about money matters. The benefit of having closed 100 transactions is that you are seasoned in solving many kinds of intricate problems that can kill a deal. A property feature might be the deck, but you would sell the benefit of the deck as a place to enjoy barbecues with friends and family; the fireplace is sold as a feature that provides a warm, cozy, romantic centerpiece for those cold winter nights.

However, these features are only benefits if your clients are interested in barbecues or romance. The only way to determine whether this is the case is to get to know your clients. If you don't know them well, you might spend two hours singing the praises of an outdoor barbecue to a vegetarian. Clearly, the best way to separate features from benefits is to ask questions, plain and simple. Every house has its own features. The only way to discern if the features of a particular house fit your client, is to first find out your client's needs.

Questions you might want to ask buyers include the following:

- What do you do for fun?
- Do you enjoy any sports?
- How do you spend your leisure time?
- What's important to you in a home and why?
- What kind of cooking do you like?
- What type of work do you do?
- What do your children do for fun?
- Do you have any hobbies?
- Do you have any pets?

If you're working with a seller, you are usually selling the benefits of yourself or your services. To turn features into benefits for sellers, you need to find out what problem they are trying to solve by selling their house. Questions you might want to ask sellers include the following:

- What will you do with the money you get from this house?
- What are you looking for in an agent?
- Have you sold a house before?
- If you've previously sold a house, can you describe the experience?
- What's your image of the perfect sale?
- What's your biggest fear when it comes to selling your house?

If you're talking to a for-sale-by-owner, turn features into benefits of using your services. Find out what problem they are trying to solve by selling their own house. Questions you might ask FSBOs could include the following:

- What are you trying to accomplish by selling your own house?
- What would it take for you to work with a real estate professional?
- What has been your experience with REALTORS®?
- Have you ever sold a house on your own before?

If you're talking to a seller whose listing has expired, turn features into benefits by determining what problem they are trying to solve. Questions you could ask expired listings might include the following:

- Are you still serious about selling your house?
- What would you be willing to do to get it sold?
- Do you want to avoid having your listing expire again?

Nearly every agent today recognizes that a website is an important part of a successful real estate practice. A website is crucial because according to the *2005 National Association of REALTORS® Profile of Home Buyers and Sellers*, 79 percent of home buyers used the Internet to search for homes; 21 percent of Internet home buyers found their agents online; and 75 percent of buyers who searched online drove by or looked at a home they first saw online. As time goes by, these numbers will only increase.

Obviously, the website must offer benefits, not features. One way to develop a client-focused website is to ask yourself "What do potential clients need to know?" Most people thinking about buying a home in your area will probably want to know the following things:

- What's special about the area? (schools, parks, entertainment, etc.)

- What is the difference between the various neighborhoods?
- What are things to watch out for? (home close to freeways, high-traffic areas, etc.)
- What is the price range of the homes?
- Are there any special amenities in the area?

Unfortunately, agent websites often do not sell their value to their clients. Instead, the website is all about them but there is no reason why clients would be interested in using this person. You must promote the benefit to visitors of using your services (client-focused), not just list features (agent-focused), which is why the average real estate website is usually pretty ineffective.

How do you know if your website is client-focused? Simple—just print out your home page and then highlight those points which are bona fide benefits. For example, being an agent for three years is a feature not a benefit. The benefit is what those three years do for the client, such as knowledge of your local market, experience with special challenges that your area might have, and so on. What most agents discover after this exercise is that there are few highlighted words.

You might want to seek out the services of a professional copy-writer, because writing benefit-laden copy for a website is an art and is usually well worth the money spent.

53) ASK CLIENTS FOR REFERRALS

Nearly every agent I have ever met hates cold-calling for clients, because it's frustrating, full of rejection, and fraught with peril thanks to the Telephone Consumer Protection Act, which has strict rules about who, how, and when you can call. Others find sending direct mail less threatening, but it's very ineffective and time consuming.

Wouldn't you rather be helping clients who want and appreciate your service than trying to work with the general public? You could be giving the right clients your fabulous personal service rather than spending your time listening to answering machines while cold-calling, or licking stamps for mass mailings.

Of course, the best way to get clients is by referral. People who are referred have a built-in level of trust in you because someone they know—a friend or relative—has recommended you. As a result, they are more likely to do what you ask them to do—which can only help them—and they'll be loyal to you.

Clients who are satisfied with your services want to repay you by giving you referrals. However, you need to know how to ask for them because people won't automatically refer you to their friends and family. They often forget or just get too busy.

You can't just go about asking for referrals in any old way. You have to use the proper approach or you'll face one rejection after another. First, though, assume you have the right to ask since you've worked hard for the client. Illustrate for her how important referrals are to you from the very beginning of your relationship.

Unfortunately, you cannot ask for referrals all the time because it's too pushy. No one looks forward to meeting a person who always has his hand out—the one who never talks to you unless he's asking for something. And the last thing you want to project is the impression that you are begging, which devalues you in people's eyes. How do you earn the right to ask so it doesn't sound presumptive? If you are working with a client, just do a stellar job. Wait for them to say, "Thank you," and then answer, "You're very welcome. I'm glad I could help. By the way, is there anyone else you know who could use my help?" Now most people will automatically say, "I can't think of anyone at the moment but if I do, I will definitely have them call you." If you wait for them to call, you will wait a very long time. Instead of asking in a vague way, prompt your client by being more specific about your request: "How about people at work, at church, or at the sailing club?" By asking about specific locations they frequent, clients will begin to see the faces of people they know in these groups, making it easier to come up with a prospect.

Now, if they do give you a name and phone number, what you say next is crucial.

"Thank you, I promise I will call her and let you know what happens." This terminology lets you say to the referred party, "I *promised* your friend Barbara Smith that I would give you a call. (You did promise, after all.) Is this a good time to talk?" The setup for beginning this new relationship is that you're only calling to keep a promise to her friend, which begins your relationship on a very high tone.

One note though: If you're not asking a client for a referral, if it is just someone you know, then build a relationship by becoming the person's real estate resource and providing information whenever they ask for it. Giving referrals seems like a natural step to people after someone has provided them with valuable information over time.

54) BUILD YOUR BUSINESS ON REFERRALS

If you build a large network of trusted agents to whom you can entrust your clients, you can help them no matter where in the world they are going to or coming from. Whether you have clients moving to Abilene, Alberta, or Auckland, someone in your network can help them. If they are moving into your area from Jakarta, Juarez, or Jacksonville, you can help them. A referral network can provide better service to your clients because they don't have to work with a stranger on the most important transaction of their lives, no matter where they are.

Every successful agent knows that getting referrals is the glue that keeps their business going because they're almost a guaranteed sale. And being a resource for other agents and for professional services offers your clients the power of your networking skills.

Giving an outgoing referral to another agent is beneficial to you too because you are going to be paid either a percentage or a flat fee. You do virtually no work for it and you have almost no liability. Nothing gives an agent more credibility than being referred by another agent, so the advantage to the agent receiving the referral is clear; it comes with a built-in level of trust.

Nothing could be easier than to give a referral to another agent. All you have to do is provide a name, contact number, and a little background information and you could easily earn $2,500 or more from it. If it only takes you five minutes to give one, that is the equivalent of earning $30,000 or more an hour if you all you did was give referrals all day. Again, your liability is extremely low if something goes wrong with the transaction. After all, all you did was make a recommendation to a competent agent. You didn't write a contract or make disclosures. Follow the suggestions in the above tip to get clients to refer you to their friends and families.

The obvious question is if you could make more money by representing the client yourself, why would you ever refer someone to another agent? There are several reasons:

- The client is outside your geographic area.
- The client requires expertise you don't have.
- The client's personality is not compatible with yours.
- You don't have the time for another client.
- You prefer to work with sellers and the client is a buyer.

You have to actively remind your clients and other agents that getting referrals is how you build your business. The first step toward convincing other agents to send you people is to begin with the ones in your area. To do this you must become active on your local board of REALTORS®. Attend as many meetings as you can, don't always sit with people you already know, and join a committee. Move around and meet new people to increase your networking capabilities.

You can give and get referrals by networking with people outside your area. A good resource is the REALTORS® annual state convention, where you will meet different agents from all over the state, and of course, the National Association of REALTORS® annual convention, which will bring you into contact with real estate professionals from around the world.

First, find out where new buyers in your area are moving from. For instance, many people who move to Palm Springs are coming from Los Angeles or San Francisco. (Your local chamber of commerce probably keeps statistics about where people lived before they moved to your area.) Once you know this, start targeting listing agents from those areas and ask for referrals. You want their sellers as your buyers. And this is an advantage to those who are moving because they're not moving to a strange place and then having to pick a stranger to help them. Because you've been introduced to them by someone they know, they can already feel comfortable buying a house with your guidance.

Another way to network is to attend a real estate class or seminar, and when you do, don't sit with agents from your office because you probably already get referrals from them. Better yet, attend classes outside of your local area to increase the chances of getting referrals from others.

A whole different kind of outgoing referral is not to other agents, but to professionals such as attorneys, accountants, financial planners, carpenters, electricians, and others. It's basically to anyone that your clients might need help from. If you engage in this practice regularly, you will become known as a good resource for all your clients. Expect these professionals to refer clients to you in return. If they don't reciprocate, find someone else.

And when you do give a client a referral, you need to find out periodically how the transaction is progressing. For one thing, if the referral is to another agent and the deal closes, you should expect a check. For another, when clients go along with your recommendation to work with a professional on their house, they are putting their trust in you to steer them in the right direction. They're investing time and money in this person on your say-so. They expect competent service and honest treatment. They assume they'll receive it because they don't believe you would betray their trust. That's why you have to stay on top of the transaction. If this professional is disreputable or incompetent, it will turn out to be a poor reflection on you.

Build your business on referrals and it will provide a steady stream of loyal clients for a lifetime. It will also give you more time to provide the highest value possible.

55) GIVE EVERY CLIENT AN
EFFECTIVE CLOSING GIFT

Many agents give their clients a gift at close of escrow to thank them for their business. I've talked to agents who have given gift certificates to restaurants, magazine subscriptions, barbecues, bottles of wine, and sometimes very extravagant gifts.

Unfortunately, most of these are a total waste of money because they don't serve their primary purpose: to remind clients that you are their agent for life. Ask yourself if the examples above meet this criterion. Probably not. Some agents, however, go overboard with this. One person told me that he spent $7,500 on landscaping for the buyers of a multimillion dollar home. He assured me that he more than met my requirement that a closing gift remind the clients about him. I asked him why he was so sure of himself and he half-jokingly replied, "I carved my initials into the biggest tree on the property."

How *do* you make a gift memorable? By selecting something that has special meaning for the person. For example, if you are well aware of a client's love of cooking, give her a fine Italian cookbook. Another way to make the gift a reminder is to put your name on it so that whenever clients look at it they think of you. I usually include the closing date of when they bought or sold their house.

You never want to give an expensive closing gift because this would imply that you made a great deal of money from the deal. I generally stick to the maximum that the Internal Revenue Service allows us to deduct for gifts to clients, which is currently $25. So what kind of closing gift do I give my clients? I generally give a brass and glass clock that costs me about that much. It has an inscription on the base that says, "From your agent, Michael Lee, closing date XX-XX-XX." Every time they look at the time, every time they dust it, and every time they change the battery they see my name.

While clocks work well as closing gifts for most clients, it is not appropriate for some. Asians, in particular, associate clocks with the winding down of life, so giving my usual gift to someone from this culture would be the same as saying, "I wish you were dead." Not exactly the message I want to send, so instead, I give Asians a cooking utensil set on a stand bearing the same brass plaque and inscription.

Consider giving closing gifts that reinforce your value and remind clients that you are their agent for life.

56) GUARANTEE YOUR SERVICES

If you believe in the value of your services, offer an unconditional guarantee.

Again, the services of real estate professionals are intangible, and there is little way to know how good we are until our clients try us. However, a guarantee can help relieve some of the anxiety potential clients feel when they hire us.

Guarantees have many uses in the real estate profession. The public is afraid to make a commitment because, if they make a mistake, they are stuck with it. A guarantee helps to overcome any reluctance around commitment.

One of the most common objections sellers give listing agents is "I want to think about it." However, if you guarantee them that they can cancel their listing at any time, they will have nothing to worry about because they have nothing to lose. If the transaction doesn't go well, they aren't trapped, so there's no reason not to sign with you.

Now, I know what you're thinking. "If I give people this opening, they'll cancel my listings left and right." First, you are still protected by the broker protection clause; if they end up selling their property to a buyer that you registered them with, they must still wait for 60, 90, or more days (whatever you put in the listing agreement) before doing so. This means that you are always guaranteed payment for any genuine work that you've done.

Second, few people, in my experience, will cancel their listing just because they can. In fact, in my 30-plus years in real estate, I have never had a seller who canceled for this reason. While there is certainly no guarantee that it won't happen, I promise you it is rare. The reason sellers want this option is that they're afraid they might get stuck with an agent they don't know and aren't sure they can count on. Once they see how good you really are, there's just no reason to use the option.

By the same token, some prospective home purchasers are reluctant to sign a Buyer-Broker Agreement for the same reason as sellers—they are just afraid to make a commitment. Giving them a guarantee that they can cancel at any time allows them to overcome this fear because it gives them an escape route if they are unhappy with your services.

In my experience, it's well worth using the guarantee, because you are far more likely to get clients to sign the contract. It's that simple. Perhaps a few will cancel, but many more will sign contracts with you because you have removed their fear of being trapped.

What kind of wording do I use for my guarantee? Actually, it's quite simple and goes something like this: "If the client is dissatisfied with the broker's services, the client may cancel this agreement at any time upon receipt of written notice of cancellation. Client acknowledges that the broker protection clause in the contract will apply." Obviously, you should consult your own attorney for the exact wording to use in your area.

Offering a guarantee also implies to clients that you are confident in the quality of your service. In addition, it encourages you to fulfill your promises to your clients. In this sense, a guarantee works for clients in more than just the obvious way.

If you believe you offer services of value to your client, consider guaranteeing your work. I don't think you'll be disappointed.

57) GIVE POTENTIAL CLIENTS A REASON TO CALL YOU

If you give potential clients too much information, they won't call you and they will never get the benefit of your fabulous service.

There's a delicate balance between providing enough information to be helpful and not so much that they don't need to call for more.

There are several places that this balancing act takes place. The first is in your brochure box or tube. If you put the price of your listing on the flyer outside the home, most potential buyers will not call you because they already have the information they want. Most agents recognize that when someone takes a flyer with the price on it, she rarely calls for more information but often ends up buying a house through another agent. By not giving away the price, you encourage serious buyers to pick up the phone and call. If they have to call you for the price, it's an opportunity to get them to become clients to whom you could sell either a listing from your office inventory or from the REALTORS® Multiple Listing Service.

If you doubt the impact of omitting the price from your flyers, just ask any agent who has left brochures with a price outside the house while they are holding it open. They'll tell you that most people will drive up, take a flyer, and then drive away without bothering to walk 20 feet into your open house. Some of them could have really benefited from your services, but now they will never get to know you.

When they do call, it is an opportunity for you to build a relationship with the potential clients. However, in order to accomplish this, it is imperative that you obtain their names and phone numbers. The problem is that many people are reluctant to give out their contact information because they might have to make a commitment to you as their agent—even though you could help them.

Some are just not ready to work with a REALTOR® and others think they should just look at houses on their own. This is why you need to explain to every potential home buyer how real estate agents can save them time in searching for the home of their dreams. Explain that you use every resource available to locate appropriate properties so they don't have to waste their time calling on ads in the paper.

To get people to give you their contact information when they call your office, start by introducing yourself and giving them your first name, then ask for theirs. For example, I usually say, "My name is Michael, what's yours?" Most people will reciprocate with their first names because it's not a big commitment.

Next, do not tell them what the price of the house is but ask them what kind of home they are looking for. Would they prefer a one- or two-story house? How many bedrooms and baths do they need?

If the property meets their needs, tell them that the house sounds perfect for them and you would like to set up an appointment to show it to them. Then simply say, "What phone number can I call you back at?"

If the property doesn't meet their needs, let them know that you have access to other properties that do, and make a special point of the fact that you are saving them time. Then just say, "At what phone number can I contact you?"

Another way we often give too much information to clients is in our farming handouts. My handout is called "What's Going on in the Neighborhood" and lists various properties that have sold recently in the area. We must realize that when a real estate agent is standing on a home owner's doorstep there is only one thing the home owner wants from us—to know what her house is worth. However, I do not include the addresses of sold houses, only the street name. This way, if clients want to know the exact address of a particular property, I will have to call them back with that information.

If I'm door-knocking and the owner is not home, I just leave a flyer and if they want to know the address, they have to call me. This is another opportunity for me to convert callers to clients and provide the exact information that will meet their needs.

Yet another way we let business slip though our fingers is in our ads and websites. If you put the price or address of your listings in your ads, potential clients have no reason to call you. Find a way to always leave some crucial piece of information out of your marketing materials to encourage clients to contact you.

DEVELOP AND MAINTAIN A BLOG

A Weblog, otherwise known as a *blog*, is a guided discussion about a particular topic. For clients, your blog information enables them to learn about your area and your expertise without having to make a commitment until they're comfortable with you. For real estate agents, it is an effective way to begin a discussion with potential clients about their local area. It is also a great tool for building rapport and credibility within your geographic area.

A blog is nothing more complicated than an online discussion board, and you don't even have to write it yourself. Usually you just have to put forth an interesting question that invites comments and that gets the ball rolling. Because the blog is under your name, the increasing volume of hits gives you more credibility. It is an invaluable tool for posting information and asking questions for people to read and possibly make comments about. Your blog can be a valuable "meeting place" for potential buyers and sellers to air their questions and bring up their worries.

There are a number of benefits to developing and maintaining a blog:

- Blogs let potential clients know and trust you in a short amount of time. They allow you to demonstrate your expertise and knowledge in a very conversational format.
- Blogs are much easier to write, publish, and deliver than newsletters. Since they are nothing more than your thoughts and responses to visitors' comments and questions, the postings can be extremely short, perhaps only a paragraph or two. You can publish them by just posting them rather than having to create a layout as is required with a written newsletter.
- Visitors come to you, so there are no spam filters like those that block your newsletters.
- It can improve the Web ranking of your website. Search engines love the fresh content found on a blog because you are (hopefully) updating it on a regular basis.

You need to carefully target your audience. Just make sure that the entire content of the blog has relevance to the people who are buyers or sellers in your area. Who are you trying to attract? Is it primarily sellers or buyers? Is it owners or buyers of commercial or investment properties? This enables you to customize the content to your audience.

To get started, you will need a hosting service such as www.blogger.com or www.typepad.com. These and others are quite easy to set up and use. Choose a domain name that incorporates the name of your service area; for example, www.gothamcitynews@blotspot.com. Don't forget that you should register a unique blog domain name and that you can link it to your website.

The real key to making your blog effective is to have current and appropriate content. Ask yourself, "What does my audience want and need to know about my area?" One of the easiest ways to do this is to have a list of frequently asked questions, answer them, and then solicit more from readers. It is a kind of self-perpetuating discussion.

Not only selling agents can use blogs to their advantage. Listing agents are now doing the same to solicit comments about their listings. This helps to give their sellers a buyer's-eye view of what people really think about their property. High-tech agents have received comments such as these on their blogs:

- "The house shows okay but is the seller serious about the price? It's at least fifty thousand dollars higher than anything similar I've seen!"
- "The house should be repainted in more neutral colors. I'm sure the seller enjoyed the color scheme while they lived there, but not everyone enjoys purple and yellow walls."
- "There's way too much furniture in such a small house. It made me feel cramped and claustrophobic."

Not only do these comments help agents, they're great for buyers and sellers too. These people are immediately put in touch with the reality of buying and selling a home. It might well keep them from making mistakes or bad decisions that cost them time and money.

Keep in mind that comments are almost always submitted anonymously, which makes it easy for oddballs to write up a storm. However, they are enormously helpful for agents and clients to spot trends. Use them to make your point with clients by selecting the ones that reinforce just the point you've been trying to make. It will encourage people to take your suggestions and make the transaction go faster.

Be sure to update your blog on a regular basis. There are easy ways to do this, and you can even post audio segments remotely from anywhere in the world.

59) BE UNIQUE. SEPARATE YOURSELF FROM YOUR COMPETITION

If you are not unique, it will be difficult for consumers to pick you out from the crowd. So be different by embracing and advertising the special qualities you possess that will benefit your clients. You might have expertise such as speaking another language, have an interesting background, or just have a highly unusual hobby. Make sure that potential clients are aware of your uniqueness by promoting it in all your marketing. Who knows when you'll point out something that creates a sense of kinship with someone.

No matter what interests you have or skills you have developed, there are clients who will appreciate what you have to offer. For example, you might collect antique cars or grow tropical plants. Obtain a roster of similar-minded people from a list broker and write a letter that speaks their language and communicates to them that they will be able to relate to you easily. You can also find providers of targeted lists in the Yellow Pages or on the Internet under *list brokers*. Then ask for their "list of lists," which tells you the categories of people they provide information about.

Make sure your advertising has its own brand. Don't offer a "free competitive market analysis," for instance, because everyone else does that, and sellers already know that most agents will provide this for free, the same as you. It's like a supermarket bragging that they give out free bags with their groceries. It would make people roll their eyes. What you want to promote, however, is any special expertise you have, and then describe how it can benefit them. It's probably wise to hire a professional copywriter to help you develop effective ads. This would be especially beneficial for your personal brochures. Most people don't realize how difficult it is for us to write about ourselves in a way that doesn't sound egotistical, self-centered, and self-aggrandizing. We also don't know how to present ourselves in the best possible light using strong, communicative language.

If everyone else uses white open house signs, try using red or yellow to make yours stand out from the herd. You might even add balloons or streamers if they are allowed in your area.

I know an agent who makes his business cards just slightly (about one-sixteenth of an inch) larger than standard cards. Not only does his stand out in a stack of cards, but he wins more raffles with his business card than the average agent.

Constantly look for ways to separate yourself from the competition. Remember, if you do what everyone else does you will get what everyone else gets, which is not much.

60) BE AWARE OF WHAT OTHER AGENTS ARE OFFERING SO YOU CAN PROVIDE MORE

Many agents hate to receive advertising from other agents. Personally, I love it! Most of the time it's all the same, but every once in a while I'll see something unique and I'll put it in a file folder. When I'm doing similar outreach to clients, I will take whatever ideas appeal to me (you can't copyright an idea) from the folder and incorporate them into my marketing. This ensures that I am doing all I can for my clients, above and beyond what other agents are doing.

To create value for yourself, don't list the same features everyone else does. Avoid the following, for instance:

- Free market analysis
- Hard work
- Superior service
- Integrity
- Knowledge of the local market

What can you give your clients that is out of the ordinary? Consider offering reports on your website that they can download for free. All they have to do is provide their email address. Such reports could include the following:

- How to Choose a Real Estate Agent
- How to Get Your House Ready to Sell
- How to Buy the Home of Your Dreams
- Choosing the Best Home Loan
- Financing the Home of Your Dreams
- Avoiding Taxes When Selling Investment Property
- What Is Title Insurance and How Does It Protect You?

Much of the information for these reports is available from lenders, title companies, attorneys, and elsewhere, but you have combined it into one easy-to-read brochure for the readers' convenience.

Develop a profile of the kinds of people who seem to be attracted to you and target them with your marketing. Are they younger or older, males or females, professionals or blue collar? This is not to say that you should discriminate against any of the federally protected groups—race, creed, color, religion, sex, national origin, age, disability, veteran, or sexual orientation. We should all strive to provide our services equally to all consumers. However, it is to everyone's benefit for you to spend the majority of your time with people, whenever possible, who you can relate to. It makes for a mutually beneficial working relationship right from the start.

61) DIFFERENTIATE BETWEEN "WHAT WE SELL" AND "HOW WE SELL"

What we sell is real estate. The problem is that a lot of people sell real estate, and being just another agent moves us toward becoming another one of those commodities which are only differentiated by price. *How* we sell is what makes us different and valuable to our clients.

You don't need to be all things to all people. You just need to be valuable to the people who can appreciate you.

We all sell real estate differently and by putting our own unique touch and personalities into our work, we increase our value. Some of us are known for being very caring and supportive, and this tends to be most appreciated by people who are involved in the helping professions like nursing and teaching. Others of us are very analytical and numbers-oriented, and this tends to attract clients such as engineers and accountants.

You must recognize that clients are drawn to you because of how you sell and who you are. These are the people who will appreciate your value; the rest you should refer to agents who are more appropriate for them.

Capitalize on how you sell by using the most powerful word for your clients in your advertising. For instance, you would never use the word *feelings* if you are trying to market to analytical types. Likewise, you would rarely use the word *subsidize* when talking to a teacher.

Your personal style is part of everything you do—from the car you drive to the way you dress to the way you conduct yourself in the real estate profession. If your style is unique, a select group of people will be drawn to you. You will have a quicker and stronger rapport with these folks because there is a subtle kinship and similarity in your styles.

How you sell is also represented by your whole demeanor around the home buying or selling process. Some agents are very businesslike and efficient while others are more casual and laid-back. Some are brash and aggressive while others are more quiet and subdued. One is not necessarily better than the other, but again, they are different and are appreciated by different types of clients.

Some agents are very factual while others try to appeal to the emotions. Each approach appeals to a different group of clients.

Be clear on how you sell and how you are perceived by clients. Capitalize on your appeal, and refer any client who does not appreciate the unique value you bring to our profession.

62) DEVELOP A FABULOUS "ELEVATOR SPEECH"

Almost everyone in business knows what this is. An *elevator speech* is an explanation of what you do for a living that can be given to people in 30 seconds or less—because you never know when you will run into a potential client. If someone walked into an elevator with you and asked, "What do you do for a living?" Would you have a well-rehearsed answer before one of you got off at their floor?

This speech not only quickly differentiates you from your competitors and establishes you as a brand, it also helps you succinctly convey the specific benefits of working with you as opposed to someone else. Your spiel should also make it clear to people what kinds of clients you work with and which ones you don't. An effective speech has the following five elements:

1. It is short.
2. It is clear.
3. It grabs attention.
4. It promotes your benefits, not your features.
5. It is unique.

For example, I would tell people: "I sell houses for more than owners thought they'd get, and buy houses for less than clients thought they'd pay." If they want to know more, I explain that I'm a broker who loves to negotiate everything from house prices to discounts on gas for my car. Anyone can do the paperwork, but very few people have earned a black belt in negotiation, and it is sharp negotiating that brings in the winning deal. My clients always feel they got the best deal possible. It isn't often that people turn away from that without asking a question or two. If they want to know how I do this, I elaborate on my background in finance, taxation, marketing, and bargaining. I might even bring out a copy of another book I have written, *Black Belt Negotiating* (AMACOM Books, 2007).

The perfect pitch makes people want to stay in the elevator to hear more. It is a conversation starter that you've practiced and honed, yet it shouldn't sound rehearsed.

Think about your elevator pitch. Is it short? Cut out any word that does not create impact. Is it clear? Put yourself in the other person's shoes and ask yourself if you know what the speech was about. Is it unique? Does it sound original or does it sound like something you've heard before? Does it grab people's attention? If the points are generic and boring, go back to the drawing board. Is it client-focused and geared toward benefits, not toward agent features? Make sure the other person understands what you will be doing for him.

This final point is your ultimate goal: tell people what you can do for them, don't talk about yourself. One of the key obstacles job counselors have to overcome with young prospects who are going to interviews, is that they want to go in and talk about what they are interested in. They have to be taught to focus on the company they want to work for and accentuate how much value they will bring to the company if they're hired. The same applies to you.

Try your elevator speech out on a couple of people and ask for their feedback. Start with friends and relatives and then move up to past clients. When you're ready, start practicing it on strangers, in elevators, and elsewhere.

Again, the test of whether it is effective is whether or not people ask you for more information about real estate and whether some of them eventually become clients. Keep improving your speech to make it shorter, more client-focused, and more effective. Try changing some of the words so they'll have more impact. Take the key words and look for more powerful synonyms for them. Eliminate unnecessary or ineffective words, and continually try to make your elevator pitch shorter. Briefer is always better because they keep making those elevators faster. Have people try to feed back to you what they heard you say. If they can't remember it after hearing it once, you still have work to do.

63) ESTABLISH A PHYSICAL FARM

Having an area of homes that you market to on a regular basis is generally called a *farm* in the real estate industry. A *physical farm* is one consisting of houses, as opposed to a *social farm*, which consists of people. It can be a tremendous benefit to clients because you become the expert for both buyers and sellers. If someone in the farm wants to sell, you know the competition and exactly how to highlight the benefits of living in the area. If someone wants to buy in the farm, you know the inventory, schools, and all the other amenities it offers.

To start a farm, choose an area of 400 to 500 homes that is near your home or office (if it's out of your way to go there, you probably won't). You want a farm that is convenient because you want to be able to walk or drive through on a regular basis. This way, you will probably see home owners fixing up their properties and homes that are in disrepair, which are indications that owners may be interested in selling in the near future.

Find different ways to contact the owners of homes in your farm such as knocking on doors, sending mailings, leaving door hangers, hosting a garage sale for the neighbors, or other techniques for building a relationship with them. Obviously, you should be familiar with local door-knocking laws and the safety precautions for doing this in your area.

Probably the biggest mistake agents make when selecting a farm is that they set their sights on the most expensive homes in the area because the commissions will be larger. While this may be true, what most agents fail to recognize is that the turnover rates on these properties is very low. On average, a home in the United States is sold every eight years. However, starter properties such as condominiums, town homes, and small houses turn over much more rapidly. These owners only keep them three to five years on average before moving up to a larger property. This means that for the same number of homes in a farm, you will get two to three times the turnover for starter properties compared to the median priced homes in your area. The higher priced properties turn over less often than average—probably only once every 12 to 15 years—you would need about 50 percent more high priced properties in your farm to equal the turnover rate of median priced homes. And don't forget that because of their high prices, owners of more expensive properties are more likely to try to reduce your commission.

If you decide to physically knock on doors, have something to give the occupants, such as a flyer of a new listing in the area or a list of homes in the area that have sold. Remember, don't put the exact address of any property on your list, but rather just give the street name, number of bedrooms and baths, square footage, closing date, and the sales price. Why do you want to omit the addresses? Once again, if you give people this information, they won't need to ask you to find out exactly where it is.

Keep good records when you farm. It's unlikely that anyone whose doorbell you ring will give you an immediate listing, but many will give you a reason why, in a year or two, they might sell. Note this in your computer or other record-keeping system, get permission to call or email them periodically, and be sure to stay in touch on a regular basis.

Also, don't be discouraged by owners who say, "I'm never going to sell. They'll have to carry me out of here in a pine box." Life changes fast. If you don't stay in touch with them, the very next week you might see a "For Sale" sign on their property and think they lied to you—but they may have gotten a job transfer or suddenly become ill. Nobody knows the hand they'll be dealt next.

64) WRITE ARTICLES FOR YOUR LOCAL NEWSPAPER

Writing real estate articles about your local area can establish you as an expert and increase your value as an agent. Clients want to work with a real estate expert, and being a local celebrity is an added bonus. You will likely find that they clip your articles and show them to their friends, saying, "*My* agent wrote this."

Being a published author can also get your name out to people who need the special services you have to offer. If they're looking for an agent and read an article by you that reassures them you are what they're looking for, you have just saved them a lot of time.

Look for new developments, construction or demolition that is going on, and anything else even remotely real estate related in your area. Do your research and then contact your local paper and offer them your article on any subject that might affect the community or the marketplace.

Some of the subjects newspapers are often interested in running are the following:

- How to choose a real estate agent
- How law changes impact the local community
- How to buy a home in a sellers' market
- How to sell a home in a buyers' market
- How to stage a home to look its best
- How to price a home so it sells
- How various bond measures will affect the real estate market
- How a rent control ordinance might affect your market
- How a new planned development might affect your market

- Are foreclosure rates increasing or decreasing?
- How to negotiate a short sale with a lender

Any of these subjects will provide useful information for the public at large and for potential clients.

The more customized an article is for your local market, the better the newspapers like it. If you demonstrate that you can write a series of real estate articles, they like it even more. I've even had newspapers ask for a continuing real estate column on various subjects.

You probably won't get paid much to write these articles. However, the visibility you receive will be priceless, and being a published author increases your value in the minds of potential clients. Try giving out articles instead of business cards because they certainly say more about you and your level of expertise. Include them with your resume because they're as powerful as testimonial letters.

Once you've written an article, even if it isn't formally published in your local paper, put it on your website as a resource. If the information is applicable to an audience beyond your local area, consider offering it to your state association of REALTORS® magazine and even the National Association of REALTORS® magazine. Don't forget that many real estate groups have state and national magazines, including the Women's Council of REALTORS®, the Council of Residential Specialists, and many others. There are also real estate websites that carry articles by agents and brokers.

Don't worry if you're not the world's most experienced writer. Local papers especially don't expect Ernest Hemingway for this kind of work. If you're brief and to the point, and if you write the way you speak, you will do a perfectly fine job. The newspaper will probably assign an editor to make sure your writing conforms to their standards.

Don't forget to send in comments to the op-ed column of your local newspaper, in addition to all the aforementioned magazines. They are always running real estate related editorials since real estate can be a very controversial subject. Unfortunately, it seems that the majority of editorials are anti–real estate, so we as professionals need to respond to these as soon as we see them. Write with passion and support your position with as many facts as your local board can supply you with. Don't forget, we're all in this together.

65) HAVE A MARKETING PLAN THAT BRINGS MORE BUSINESS THAN YOU NEED

If you are always looking for new business, you won't have time to adequately service your current clients. If you run out of clients, you will be out of business and all the clients who could have benefited from your experience and knowledge will be left with lesser agents. If you are always worried about where your next commission is coming from, this distraction will keep you from providing the best possible care to your clients.

Too many agents think their job is to sell real estate. In reality, it is to build their business. There is a certain built-in insecurity in this business because once a client uses your services, he might not need them again for a long time. You have to keep drumming up new business or you won't have a business. You need a good marketing plan that brings you consistent business year after year. Consider this: You will lose 10 to 15 percent of your clients every year just because some move away, some will go with other agents no matter how good you are, and some die. If you don't replenish your supply of clients, within six to seven years or so, you will be out of clients.

Choose a marketing technique that you actually enjoy so you will implement it consistently. Here are just a few of the best ways to obtain buyers and sellers:

- **Sphere of influence farming:** Stay in touch with friends, family, and former coworkers on a regular basis. These people already know and trust you, so just keep reminding them that you are in the real estate profession.
- **Social farming:** Get involved in a social organization that can bring you into contact with qualified buyers and sellers of real

estate in your area. Such groups could be the local PTA, golf clubs, yacht clubs, or ski clubs.

- **Holding houses open:** Open houses attract buyers and some sellers. While the chances of someone walking into an open house and buying that house are statistically low, many of the visitors are qualified buyers who could become your clients.

- **Contacting absentee owners:** People who are renting out houses often don't like the property management hassles and might be ready for either professional property management or selling the property. Many do not sell because they don't want to pay the capital gains tax. Educate them about doing an Internal Revenue Service Code Section 1031 exchange, which can defer the taxes.

- **Physical farming:** Establish a farm of homes in your area that you contact on a regular basis. It could be based on geography, property type, or another category. See Tip #63.

- **Wearing career apparel:** This is clothing that has the REAL-TORS® "R" or the name of your company on it. After owning and managing hundreds of agents, I've found that if you wear career apparel on a regular basis, you will get two to four extra transactions a year as a result of the increased visibility. The other terrific thing about career apparel is that people will come up to you and ask you about real estate rather than you having to sell yourself to them.

- **Contacting for-rent-by-owners:** Many people who are renting out houses generally don't like being in the rental business. If they only have one rental house, they may currently be experiencing 100 percent vacancy. Their previous tenants may have damaged the property, causing them lost time and expenses in repair before they could even put it on the rental market.

66) MEET YOUR BEST CLIENTS FACE-TO-FACE

Who are your "best clients"? First off, and of primary importance, they're the ones who bring you the most business. (There are also personal considerations, which we will cover later in the book.) One of the most basic rules of real estate is "All clients are not created equal." In other words, some clients are more important than others. Eighty percent of any business's profits, according to the Perito Principle, will come from 20 percent of its customers. This has been proven true over and over in various industries, not the least of which is real estate. Your goal is to find a way to come face-to-face with the top 20 percent of clients, and to do it on a regular basis, because that will solidify your relationship with these "rainmakers."

First, of course, you have to identify who the rainmakers are. At the end of each year, track your closed transactions back to the source. You are looking for the clients from whom you have directly earned commissions, and for clients who have referred other clients to you, or any other people—like accountants, attorneys, contractors, or other agents—who brought you business. Put their profiles into a separate database so you can contact them whenever necessary.

Next, find a way to meet with these people face-to-face at least once a year. Try to think outside the box when considering how you want to do this. Don't just call them into your office for coffee in a Styrofoam cup. (How many do you think would show up?) Do something enticing like holding a party or taking them all on a cruise or entertaining them in a private box at a ball game. Look for any excuse to remind them that they are special and that you are their agent for life.

An annual event keeps you at the top of their minds. In general, you will want to contact these people in other ways at least four times a year; the annual event is just one of those contacts.

Don't forget, a lot of other agents are competing with you. This is, and always has been, a very crowded market. What are you willing to do to make yourself part of your clients' lives so that the minute they even think of buying or selling a house, you are the only one they consider contacting? The best analogy I can think of here is the family doctor. Once Mom and Dad have built up a sense of trust with him or her, it doesn't occur to them to call anyone else when little Elsie comes down with the chicken pox. You want to become similarly trusted. You want to be the one they call for real estate related matters.

Be sure to schedule your meeting at a time when most people are available, so avoid the traditionally busy times of the year such as Thanksgiving, Christmas, New Year's, and Labor Day.

Here are just a few ideas from successful agents around the country about how they get face-to-face time with their best clients every year:

- Robert Geary in Rhode Island holds a holiday pie giveaway around mid-December at a local bakery. He sends certificates to his best clients and asks them to come in to pick up their pies between 5:00 P.M. and 8:00 P.M. on a specific day. Coffee and tea are available so they can stay a while and even enjoy a piece of pie while they chat with him. Robert says that a lot of his clients love this idea because they don't have time to bake around the holidays and the pies come in handy. And those who are not able to pick up a pie are appreciative anyway and will often call to thank him, which gives him a chance to catch up and ask for referrals.

- Anna Davis in Texas has a kids' holiday event to make tree decorations in early December. She brings all kinds of materials for ornaments such as Styrofoam balls, plaster, glitter, glue, paint, and such. There are games and videos to occupy the kids while the parents can go Christmas shopping unimpeded for a couple of hours.

- Jim Gurman in California has a beer-brewing party during the summer, where his clients help make the beer, swim, and eat. Six months later, it's time to have another party to drink the now-ready beer and toast old friends.

67) GET INVOLVED WITH A
LOCAL CHARITY

Nothing says value to a client more than seeing their agent giving back to the community through a local charity. While being involved in a nonprofit organization certainly takes time away from your business, it can become part of your marketing plan so you don't feel guilty about devoting energy to it.

Find a charity that you can feel good about supporting, and get involved. If you have pictures taken of you hard at work volunteering, it promotes you and your company, and it shows potential clients that you are truly involved in the community you serve as an agent. Becoming involved with a local charity tangibly and visibly demonstrates your value to clients and to the community, because you are participating in events and situations that have nothing to do with real estate. Consider chairing various fund-raising efforts such as golf tournaments, charity auctions, casino nights, and other activities.

Encourage agents from your office to get involved by explaining how much it has added to your life. One of the main benefits of charitable involvement can be to provide networking opportunities with high income and high profile people.

There are thousands of worthy groups across the country. Habitat for Humanity, the American Cancer Society, Greenpeace, and the American Red Cross are only a few. All of these provide services and value for local communities and the world at large.

Before getting involved, learn all you can about the organization and the people it serves. Obviously, you want to make sure it's legitimate and not some kind of scam, so ask to see a copy of their Internal Revenue Service Code Section 501(c)(3) letter. This status allows people who donate funds to the organization to potentially deduct the contribution from their taxes.

After verifying the legitimacy of the group, go out and meet some of the people who have been helped by the organization. This will show you in a direct way where the money is going. Finally, ask how much of every contributed dollar goes to directly help the people they serve. Some groups spend as much as 90 percent of revenue on fund-raising and administrative expenses, leaving little for the people they are supposed to help. Look for organizations that contribute at least 50 percent of their revenue to those they're seeking to help.

Get involved in a meaningful way by volunteering, which will let you meet some of the staff. You may also wish to serve on the board of directors for the group.

Once your commitment grows, educate other agents about what services the charity provides and get them involved, as well. This will not only benefit the charity, but help you strengthen your relationships with local real estate professionals. There is nothing wrong with taking pictures of you and your office mates at these events and sending them to your local newspaper; it's a form of free advertising that lets the community know you care.

Look for opportunities to help and you never know what benefits can result. I was the chairman of the board of a credit union, and we heard that the local high school baseball team had all of their brand new equipment stolen that they had spent the entire summer raising money for. The season was about to start, so we immediately jumped into action and pulled $3,500 out of our marketing budget to pay for new gear. While never expecting anything in return except the gratitude of the players, our generosity was widely covered by local radio and television stations. As a bonus, our members barraged us with calls saying how proud they were that *their* credit union had been so thoughtful. It appears that good news does sell!

68) CONDUCT CUSTOMER SATISFACTION SURVEYS

One of the most tangible ways to differentiate yourself from your competitors and prove your value to clients is to let others tell them how good you are. A survey is a great tool for that because it lets prospects know what your clients thought of your services.

You can conduct a survey yourself or hire a company to develop one, but do it after every closed transaction. They should be conducted within two weeks following close of escrow, so that the experience of buying or selling will still be fresh in the client's mind; they will be more likely to answer the questions at this point.

A professional survey implies greater impartiality and credibility than conducting your own. People are also more likely to respond to a survey and be more candid in it if they know it won't come directly back to you.

Surveys can be conducted by phone, online, or in writing through mail, but phone surveys seem to be the most effective. Your response rate on mailed surveys is likely to be extremely slow, whereas those conducted by phone have a quicker turnaround.

Surveys can provide you with valuable information about your clients as well as how they feel about the quality of your services. They let you know what areas of improvement you need to focus on or what new services you should be offering. You can also find out what clients thought of your closing gifts and get feedback on how you handled any problems that arose during the transaction.

An effective customer satisfaction survey should not only measure critical success factors such as responsiveness, knowledge of the market, and understanding of the client's needs, but should also measure the client's perceptions of the agent. You want to make sure that you are not only meeting, but exceeding, client expectations. The results of the survey might not benefit the person who is answering the questions, but the improvements you make as a result of those answers will most certainly benefit future clients.

Surveys should also capture client loyalty data. You can ask such questions as "How likely are you to use this agent again?" or "How likely are you to recommend this agent to others?" Remember, you are trying to build a list of clients for life and surveys are one component of that plan.

If you are going to use any quotes from customers in your marketing materials, be sure you get permission from the person first. I also get permission to use my clients' pictures next to their quotes.

Few ads for real estate agents are more powerful than those in which clients themselves are praising our abilities.

For it to be effective, you must get a high percentage of clients to complete your survey. Here are some ways to increase your response rate:

- Be sure your questions are relevant to your clients. It's probably best to have separate questions for buyers and sellers since your work for each is very different.
- Let your clients know how the survey will benefit them, such as helping you improve your service to all your clients.
- Let them know from the start that you will be asking them to complete a survey after escrow closes.
- Let clients know how important customer satisfaction is to you.
- Make your survey easy and quick to complete.
- If mailed, include a postage-paid, pre-addressed return envelope.
- Provide a fax number in case clients want to return it that way.
- Give an incentive for clients to complete the survey, such as an entry in a contest or other reward.
- Have a third party follow up on all unreturned surveys by phone.

69) BRAND YOURSELF

A brand is the effect that your name, logo, slogan, and other collateral materials have on the public. When you have a brand, it means that whenever anyone hears your name they immediately think of real estate. Branding reaches people at a deep emotional level. It is the feeling people get when they look at your name or picture.

To your clients, your brand is the result of the accumulation of their experiences with you which create associations and expectations in their hearts and minds. It's how they perceive you as a whole. While this is relatively easy to define on paper, it's extremely difficult to create.

When people think of a company that has a distinct brand, right away Disneyland comes to mind. Its brand is that it is fun for kids and provides a safe, wholesome environment for the whole family. The image starts with its slogan, "the happiest place on earth," and continues through every aspect of the experience it provides. The pancakes are shaped like Mickey Mouse and workers are dressed as cartoon characters to act as greeters. There are lots of theme parks in the world, but no one confuses any of them with Disneyland.

Unfortunately, most real estate professionals do not have a brand that stands out nearly as well. It might not be possible to be known around the world, but we can certainly become celebrities in our own areas. One way to accomplish this is to become visible by employing various techniques. Write a column for your local newspaper (see Tip #64), host a local radio or television real estate show, and gain visibility participating in a charity event (see Tip #67). Creating a brand is not advertising per se, but it can certainly support it.

Here are just a few aspects that can go into branding yourself so you are known as a real estate professional:

- Impeccable ethics
- Expert knowledge
- Quick responses
- Smart showing style
- High-class fashion sense
- Evenhanded and smooth manner of speech
- Masterful problem solving
- Pleasant disposition
- Charming personality
- Consummate professionalism
- Unique differentiation from competition

The key to developing a recognized local brand is consistency. The service you deliver must be consistent day and night, weekdays and weekends, in sickness and in health. Even when you're having a bad day, you can't let it carry over to the client. If they know you as a calm, nice person, you can destroy that in a moment with a sudden outburst of temper. If they know you as businesslike and professional, you can lose your reputation by disclosing something personal about another client that was certainly meant to be private. Consistency also means that you are always there to solve their problems—even when you aren't there. One way to provide consistency of service when you are ill, on vacation, or otherwise unavailable is to have another trusted agent stand in your place. Many people I know have an agreement with an agent in their office that they'll handle their clients when they are away and vice versa. The type and number of clients you both have should be similar so no one feels abused by handling too much of the load. By applying many of the principles in this book, you can develop a well-recognized local brand that will differentiate you from your competitors, make you remembered by your past customers, attract new customers, and sell your value to current clients.

70) GUARD YOUR REPUTATION AT ALL COSTS

Because real estate is a service business, your reputation is a vital part of your value. Your good reputation is a composite of the benefits that are associated with your name. It is all the emotions and images that clients have when they hear about you. Unfortunately, there are a few unscrupulous agents who hurt the reputation of all of us by taking advantage of the trust of their clients.

Reputation and brand are very different. A brand is the experience you provide to your clients and the emotions that are called to mind around this experience. When people hear your name, do they feel pleased, satisfied, and comfortable? On the other hand, reputation is the sum of the beliefs, assumptions, and perceptions about how you operate and what you stand for. Do clients believe, assume, and perceive you to be ethical, knowledgeable, and honest?

Why is a positive reputation important to a real estate professional? It helps to build trust and create value with clients and potential clients. When a transaction is weighed down with challenges, clients won't automatically assume you've made a mistake or that you're trying to cheat them as long as you have a reputation for competence and fair dealing.

It's vitally important that if you hear negative comments made about you from others, you take immediate action to correct any erroneous information. This is known as reputation management. This does not mean that you become hypersensitive to the slightest derogatory comment because, when you are successful, you become a magnet for jealous people who want to defame you. However, if there are factual errors made about your practices, you must address them immediately. This tells others that you value your reputation enough to insist that accusations be proven.

Your reputation is built one client at a time over years, by being consistently ethical and reliable. More than anything, it is important to leave people feeling that you are, at the very least, competent. Even if you're really, really good, you'll be lucky if a client tells two or three other people. However, if you provide incompetent service, statistics say the dissatisfied customer will tell 12 people.

A carefully cultivated reputation is worth its weight in gold. People pay more for brand name products than for the equivalent generic item because they know what to expect when they open the package. For them, saving a few cents just isn't worth the disappointment of receiving an inferior product. If people have heard about you before they meet you, and what they heard is uniformly positive, they will be willing to pay more because they feel sure you are worth it. Build your reputation carefully and guard it well because it's worth a lot of money. You will be able to command a higher fee than generic agents and you will receive more referrals as well.

71) LEARN TO NETWORK LIKE A PRO

Networking gives you access to additional resources, skills, and knowledge, all of which serve your client. It's nothing more than meeting people, developing relationships, and then maintaining those relationships. Despite all the excitement over technology, you must remember that real estate is still a contact sport. All computers, PDAs, email, and websites can do is attract potential clients and make the paperwork a bit easier, but ultimately a closed transaction comes down to building relationships with clients. You must come face-to-face with potential and current clients to build a successful real estate practice.

Find places such as the following where you can meet new clients:

- Chambers of commerce meetings
- Your church
- Community groups
- Civic groups such as Rotary or the Elks
- The golf course
- Alumni associations

Don't forget that real estate clients can include professionals such as accountants, attorneys, financial planners, and others, so look for opportunities to meet and network with them as well. Here are some helpful hints for networking at meetings:

- Stand near the door or the food table to meet the maximum number of people.
- Introduce yourself first. People assume you are friendly when you take the initiative.
- Smile—it immediately breaks the ice.
- Have your elevator speech ready (see Tip #62).
- Offer help without any expectation of return. The other person may want to know the status of a building for sale in her area or just be curious about current interest rates.
- Have plenty of business cards handy, but always get the other person's contact information first.
- If you have a difficult name to pronounce, find a way to make it easy for the other person. For example, if your name is

Shoeflekey, you might say "shuffle-key" and do a little dance with your keys in your hand as you say it. Trust me, they won't forget you.

- Follow up after the event with a brief handwritten note.
- If you promise to call or provide information, be sure to do so.
- Ask questions about the other person. If there is anything people like talking about, it's themselves.

Too many agents put themselves under undue pressure thinking they have to drum up business wherever they go. Remember that your objective is simply to meet as many people as you can. You want to see if you like a person and if he is compatible with you (see Tip #77). Then you need to determine if the person has an immediate real estate need. If not, just stay in touch with him until he does.

Make an effort to network on a regular basis. It should be an integral part of your marketing plan.

72) BE UNIQUE WITH YOUR OPEN HOUSES

Potential home buyers will remember you if you offer perks that no one else does. For instance, if average agents hold their houses open on Sundays from 1:00 P.M. to 4:00 P.M., consider holding yours open a half hour earlier and later, say, from 12:30 P.M. to 4:30 P.M. The earlier opening time gives you a chance to catch people coming home from church, as well as agents going to their own open houses. The later closing time lets other agents, who are finishing at 4:00 and coming home from their own open houses, view your property after they've completed their other duties. Because your listing is still open, they now have the opportunity to give it a look-see without the distraction of the hordes. In addition, you're giving a lot of buyers— who cannot view any other properties because they are closed—the chance to see one more. This window of opportunity greatly benefits your clients because it opens that very small viewing window just a little wider. Since you are going to make flyers and drag your open house signs out anyway, you might as well stay an extra hour.

If average agents put out two or three open house signs, you use five or six to bring in people to your listing from a wider area. I know one agent in my area who puts out at least 30 open house signs every Sunday. It takes two guys with two flatbed trucks two hours to set out and pick up her signs! While this might seem like overkill, she claims that the practice lets her sell 85 percent of her own listings. While I'm not advocating that every agent do the same thing, it certainly makes her unique in her market area.

However, one open house practice that upsets the public and has even led to legislation in some areas is the custom of placing a sign at busy street intersections, even though several others are already there. This results in an unsightly and totally unnecessary "sign farm," and it could even pose a hazard if it slows down traffic. If several signs are already pointing in the same direction as your open house, why not just let them attract the traffic? I guarantee you, once people are already headed in your direction and see your sign in front of the house, they will look if they're interested. Only place your open house signs where it is necessary. This is simply considerate to the people living in the area. Who knows, some day they might be your clients.

73) IMPROVE CLIENT ACCESS TO YOUR WEBSITE

No matter how much time and money you spend on your website, it will be totally wasted if no one can find it. You must improve your search ranking so that you are at least in the top 10 sites in your area because few people will take the time to search beyond the most popular sites. Those who truly need your services aren't about to spend two hours looking for you.

One way to increase the ranking of your site is to have strong content. Consider writing articles about each feature that potential buyers would want to know more about. Not only will this content improve your ranking with the search engines, it will also demonstrate to visitors that you are an expert in your local area.

Amenities that most home buyers want to know more about include the following:

- Recreational areas
- Schools and academic rankings
- Year-round weather
- Parks and play areas for children
- Major employers in the area with contact information
- Cost-of-living statistics
- Hospitals and medical facilities
- Senior facilities
- Interest rate projections

Issues that most home sellers would want to know more about would include the following:

- The current real estate market in your local area
- New developments in construction or transportation that might affect their value
- Interest rate projections
- Changes in tax laws that might affect property values
- How to stage their house to obtain maximum value

Another way to raise your ranking is to select the most effective key words for the audience you are trying to reach. Be sure to include the name of the cities and specific neighborhoods that you specialize in. Ask yourself what words a potential buyer who is moving in to your area might type into a search engine.

There are many other techniques for improving your site's ranking, such as using effective title tags and HTML meta tags. If this all sounds complicated, hire consultants and companies to conduct search engine optimization for your site.

74) WRITE A POWERFUL DESCRIPTION FOR THE MLS

One of the most effective tools for getting your sellers' properties sold is the description in the multiple listing service, but most agents waste this valuable space with clichés and trite phrases. Frankly, composing this part of the marketing used to be one of my biggest challenges until I hit upon an easy solution—have the seller write it.

Today, I simply hand the owner a pad of paper and say, "We need to write a description of your property that will really grab the attention of agents and buyers. Make a list of everything you love about this house. What is special about it and what's great about the neighborhood?" I will then elaborate on her description for the multiple listing service. The seller always comes up with a far superior description than I ever could. My theory is that all the factors that brought enjoyment to the current owner are precisely what will attract potential buyers to the property.

Once I have the list from the seller, all I have to do is stack the points in order of priority to buyers and put them into the MLS. Other agents always make comments about how my MLS description seems to speak directly to their buyers. It should, because it was written by someone who is intimately familiar with all the benefits of living in the house.

Having your seller help you write the MLS description will make your life easier and your listings will sell a lot faster.

75) DEVELOP A TARGETED MARKETING PLAN FOR YOUR LISTINGS

No seller wants her house to be on the market for months at a time. Just imagine the inconvenience and disruption to her life when she has to live there in limbo, waiting for it to sell. She can't even take a soothing shower in the afternoon without taking the lock box off the front door or dead-bolting it to avoid being rudely interrupted. It's practically like living in a train station.

You can avoid this with a *targeted marketing plan*, which helps a house sell for the highest price in the shortest amount of time. Exactly what is targeting? It means developing a profile of the most likely buyer for a property and then developing a system for reaching that kind of person.

For example, if you have a condominium to sell, the most likely buyer might be young professionals with one child or no children. How do you find them? In your area, they might belong to upscale health clubs or have children in private elementary schools. Advertise in the heath club newsletters or school bulletins.

If you have an upscale estate home for sale, the most likely buyer is a professional couple with two or three children. They might belong to an exclusive golf or yacht club and have children who ride horses at the local equestrian center. Almost every golf club, yacht club, riding academy, and other group has a newsletter where you can advertise your listings. An ad in one of these outlets is likely to be far more effective than broadcasting in your local newspaper, which will mostly reach a section of the public with an average income that is far below anything that would qualify them to buy such a high-end home.

76) GET SELLERS INVOLVED IN THE MARKETING OF THEIR HOUSE

Every seller should be a partner in the marketing of his house. It's amazing how often people who are selling their house just happen to run into people interested in buying houses, all because they put the message out there. One agent I know has her business card provider print her cards on large uncut sheets. Then she has them print a couple of hundred on the reverse side with a color photo and description of every listing she takes. She gives these cards to the owners of her listings. They go to work, church, the golf course, and other places and pass them out proudly to everyone they meet. These inexpensive cards not only market the listing but also promote this smart agent, whose name, photo, and contact information are on the other side. As a bonus, while people who receive a card may not be interested in this particular listing, they could be potential buyers for other properties in the area. Guess who they call?

Other ways to get sellers involved in the marketing of their house is to ask them for a list of their friends and relatives. Contact those people to see if they know of anyone who might be interested in purchasing the property. Of course, you reference your client's name up front when calling them. Most of these people are likely to already be familiar with the impending sale, since they have probably attended parties and other functions in the house.

CLIENT SELECTION AND RELATIONS

77) WORK WITH PEOPLE YOU LIKE

Of the thousands of successful agents I have spoken with in over 30 years in our profession, the one piece of advice they consistently give me is "work with people you personally like." I think this is wise since people with whom you have an instant rapport are more likely to do those things that will result in a closed transaction. For instance, sellers who like you are more likely to lower their price or do repairs when you suggest them. Buyers you enjoy working with are more likely to look at a property or make an offer when you ask them to.

I have found that the real estate profession is difficult enough, and working with clients you don't personally like simply adds insult to injury. This is not to say that people you don't like are not honest, hardworking people, but there are some people you will have affinity for and others who just seem to rub you the wrong way.

Experience has shown that turning away a certain number of potential clients increases your credibility and value. Rejecting some

incompatible people tells the world that you don't just work with anyone and that you don't need everyone's business.

My first broker insisted that I work with every client, including
those with whom I did not have a good rapport. I remember one
couple who were very nice but with whom I had nothing in common.
In fact, I had to study the sports section of the newspaper before
meeting them so I would have something to talk about with the
husband. It's been over 20 years since I helped them buy their first
rental property—it has never had a day's vacancy and has tripled in
value. Do you think I have ever gotten one referral from this couple?
Of course not, because we never had a personal relationship, only
a business relationship. Today, my number one rule is that I must
personally like my clients, and as a result, all of my business is done
by referral. If I like them it stands to reason that the feeling is mutual,
so they are more than happy to recommend me to others.

It's okay to reject clients you don't want. In fact, turning away
clients implies that you are successful and particular. This begins to
elevate you to an agent of elite status that clients aspire to work with.
Obviously, if you are a newer agent or just happen to be experiencing a momentary slump in your business, it's difficult to turn down
clients—even if you don't happen to like them. This is why you must
have a marketing plan that brings in more potential clients than you
could ever serve (see Marketing Tip #65).

78) CHOOSE YOUR CLIENTS CAREFULLY

The power to select which client will work with which REALTOR®,
contrary to popular opinion, does not rest solely in the hands of the
client. *You* have to determine if these people are appropriate for you
as much as they must decide the same. Even if you're just starting
out, you have to be a little bit choosy. The last thing you want to
do is give off an air of desperation, which broadcasts that you have
no standards or boundaries. And if you accept everyone, some clients will be so demanding of your time that they just aren't worth

the aggravation. Personality types that don't match are a recipe for disaster because the two of you will likely never develop the rapport necessary to finish a deal. Without that rapport, clients won't take your advice and you'll be in a constant battle with each other. This is no fun for either party.

About 15 percent of buyers just want a cheap product. Do you really want to try to attract these people? The truth is that this group tends to be more trouble and less loyal than everyone else because they are really only loyal to one thing—price. Look for clients who appreciate the value of your services and are willing to pay for them. You don't need every client—just the good ones!

Do not start working with clients before asking them a series of questions to determine if they are serious and will be loyal to you. If you don't, you imply that you are desperate for clients and will do anything, including lowering your commission, to get their business.

Before making a commitment to clients, you need to determine their motivation and whether or not *you* want to work with *them*. There are many buyers and sellers who are not serious and will waste your time.

For potential sellers, you might ask the following:

- Why are you selling your house?
- What is your deadline for moving out?
- What will you do if your house doesn't sell?
- Are you interviewing any other agents?
- What's the most important factor in deciding which agent you will choose?

You are basically trying to determine their level of motivation. If you can't, the listing is likely to expire because they may not price it realistically, fix the property up, or seriously consider offers that are below their unrealistic asking price.

For potential buyers, you might ask the following:

- Why are you thinking about buying a home?
- What is your deadline for moving in?
- Have you been preapproved for a loan by a lender?
- Are you working with any other agents?
- Do you know the benefit to you of signing a Buyer-Broker Agreement?
- Have you previously made offers on any homes?

Asking a list of logical questions of potential clients not only tells them that you are a knowledgeable real estate professional, but that you care about them. It also implies that you do not just work with anyone, but you choose your clients carefully.

Have clear criteria for clients you want to serve. I have three unbreakable rules that have contributed to my success. The first rule is that they must be motivated with a clear deadline for buying or selling. The second rule is that they must respect me and the real estate profession. The third rule is that I must have an instant rapport with them. I promise, if you follow these rules you will have these clients for a lifetime.

79) SCREEN OUT UNQUALIFIED BUYERS

Working with unqualified buyers wastes their time and yours. You will get their hopes up by showing properties they cannot afford and ask them for commitment when they are not ready. You do not want to disappoint your clients.

To avoid false expectations, be sure you only work with qualified buyers who have been preapproved by a lender and who have a definite reason and deadline for buying a home. This is especially important in a buyers' market. First-time buyers may not know they can't afford a house and may launch themselves on the epic journey to buy one without any idea that it will end in failure. Nobody wants to invest their time and get their hopes up, only to be disappointed later.

One of the best ways, then, to screen out an unqualified buyer is to make sure he or she has been preapproved for a loan. Take this step before the client ever gets into your car. I explain it this way to people so they don't think I am casting aspersions on their financial status: "You might be able to afford a bigger home than you think. Why don't we find out from a lender exactly how much of a loan you will qualify for? Once we add your down payment to that, I'll know what to look for. Let's not waste your time looking in the wrong price range."

There is a process called *prequalifying* in which the buyer fills out an application. Based on this information, the lender estimates how much of a loan the borrower will qualify for. Preapproval takes prequalifying to the next level. At this stage, the borrower will not only complete the application, but will have the lender pull a credit report. Many different facts in the report can affect the amount of the loan, including credit rating, outstanding loans, delinquent loans, and more.

Sometimes buyers just aren't serious, and one clue is if they aren't willing to sit down for an hour and talk with a lender about the most important purchase of their life. Let people know why this is so crucial. They will receive a preapproval letter stating how much of a loan they are likely to qualify for, which will help any offer they make look much stronger, especially in a multiple-offer situation. I have gotten sellers to accept my client's offer—even though ours was not the highest price—just because we had a preapproval letter. It says to a seller that these buyers are serious.

80) GIVE MOTIVATED SELLERS MORE OF YOU

When you are working with a truly motivated seller, he gets your full time and attention. He is served by this, and so are you. Nobody is served by unmotivated sellers because they simply aren't serious enough to do what it takes to make their house appealing to buyers. What could they possibly get out of a deal where they aren't doing everything they can to ensure its success? When you insist that your clients put their hearts into it, you are doing them a favor. You know that in the end, they will be far more satisfied with the price they get for their home if they work for it—even if they don't know it while they are grumbling and complaining about having to strip the wallpaper off their walls and sand their floors.

Be sure, however, that you have a marketing plan that brings you more sellers than you could ever handle, so you can turn away unmotivated sellers. This is important in any market but is especially crucial in a buyers' market. The last thing you need is unmotivated sellers who take time away from the ones who need you. Rejecting a potential seller forces him to stop fooling around and make a decision. Some owners just want to "test the waters" to see if they can get what they want for their house, and what they want is almost always unrealistically high compared to what the market will bear. The faster you educate them about the realities of the market and encourage them to figure out if they are serious about selling, the better it is for everyone.

If the seller is going to successfully sell his house, he simply must be motivated. One strong motivation is to have a definite deadline for selling. A deadline is the soonest people generally do anything. Remember when you had to write an English paper in college and it was due on Tuesday a month later? When did you start it? Probably the Monday night before the due date. If there is no deadline, there is usually very little motivation to start the process. A deadline can come in the form of a job transfer, a pending bankruptcy, divorce, marriage, or moving closer to grandchildren.

Don't forget another important motivation: greed. Most people, including me, would sell their house next week if they could get far more than it was worth and make a quick profit. Unfortunately, this is not possible in most areas and in most markets. Reject sellers whose primary motivation for selling is greed because where else do you think they'll look to fatten their wallets? Your commission.

Clear signs that a seller is truly motivated are that he is willing to do the following:

- Do what you suggest to get the property ready to market including fixing up the interior, exterior, and whatever landscaping is necessary
- Take your advice about small improvements that will make a big difference in marketing
- Pay for work to be done rather than giving credits. By spending $1,500 for interior painting or to have a new carpet installed, he may avoid having to give a credit to the buyer of $5,000 or more.
- Stage the property the way you or a professional stager suggests. They accept the fact that while the house may not be comfortable during this period, it pays off in the long run because it helps the house sell faster and at a higher price.
- Have all inspections completed before the property is placed on the market. Hopefully, he trusts your experience and he'll let you do whatever you have to prevent any surprises that could kill a sale.
- Pay fair compensation for the work required to sell his house

When you tell some sellers that you don't want to work with them, your reputation and self-esteem will actually go up! Rejecting unmotivated clients tells them and the world that you have high standards and don't just work with anyone. You will also feel better about yourself because you are the one to choose the relationship, not the client. You are also doing them a favor by letting them clearly know you think they are wasting their time trying to market a property you believe will not sell.

81) NEVER LEAVE WITHOUT THE LISTING

Do you want to save your sellers a lot of grief? Help them come to the decision they already want to make but are just a bit reluctant to do.

If you do a listing presentation and leave without the listing, it is unlikely that you will ever get it. Sellers will forget what they liked about you once a certain amount of time has gone by. Or when they meet another agent, they're more impressed with him because the impression you made has faded. Don't let this happen. After you give a presentation, don't leave without the listing in hand.

This is why I like to be the last agent to do a listing presentation. No one can say, "We have to cut this short because we have another agent to talk to" or "I can't make a decision until I've spoken to everyone." In fact, I make this a requirement of my listing presentation: "I only have one request and that is that I be the last agent you talk to. The reason is that I have unique marketing techniques that you can't appreciate until you see what other agents don't have."

While many sellers have good intentions when interviewing agents, some are afraid of making a commitment to a particular agent for fear that they will get stuck with someone they're unhappy with. So they come up with all kinds of excuses for not making a decision on the spot. You must learn to deal with these excuses. Here are some common ways to get past objections and stalls:

Seller: "My neighbor said that if I was ever going to sell my house I should let her know first because she wants to buy it."
Agent: "Don't worry, we can exclude your neighbor in the listing agreement so that if she buys the property within two weeks from today, you will not owe my broker a commission."

Seller: "I need to paint (re-carpet, landscape, etc.) before I can put my house on the market."
Agent: "Terrific! It'll show much better after the work has been done. So why don't we extend our listing for three weeks and we won't show it during that time?"

Seller: "I just need to think about it."
Agent: "I certainly understand that this is a big decision. What specifically do you need to think about?"

Seller: "I need to talk to my spouse (accountant, financial advisor, etc.)."

Agent: "I know this is a big decision and I don't blame you. I do have a guarantee that if you're unhappy with my services, you can cancel the listing at any time. Why don't we sign the listing agreement and then talk to whomever you would like. If he or she doesn't think this is a good move for you, I'll be happy to cancel the listing."

82) CONTACT CLIENTS REGULARLY

Be sure to contact your clients on a regular basis. Do this even if you don't have a lot of new information to offer; it lets them know you're genuinely interested in them and value them as clients. While it may not seem like a big deal, it is, in fact, one of the biggest complaints real estate clients have about their agents.

When I begin working with new clients I always ask them how often they want me to contact them, what day of the week, what time of the day, and by what means (telephone call, email message, or faxed report). I then put this into my contact management software in my computer, and it automatically reminds me to call, email, or fax them. For instance, if a client wants a call at noon on Wednesdays, my computer will not only remind me but also dial the client's number. Nothing could be easier.

I find that one of the toughest calls I have to make is to tell a seller that there has been no new interest or offers on his house. However, relaying this bad news is far preferable to having them call me and then giving them the bad news. My regular calls give me an excuse to discuss the possibility of lowering his price, restaging the property, or other thoughts I have on new tactics for marketing the property, so the next time I call it will bring good news.

Most buyers seem to want pretty regular contact as well. They want to know if new homes have come onto the market that may meet their needs, or if their offer has been accepted by a seller. After a house goes into escrow, there are regular reports about inspections, loan approval, repairs, and hundreds of other details. If you don't keep up with your calls, you could get lost in the details.

You can also use contact management software to follow up with prospects such as potential buyers and sellers, expired listings, for-sale-by-owners, and others. Many agents fail to convert prospects to clients because they don't stay in touch. The wonders of technology can make it easy and foolproof.

83) LEARN TO DEFLECT ANGER

Buying and selling real estate can be very emotional transactions because so much money is involved. One of the most common emotions real estate professionals encounter is anger, since many things can go wrong during the course of one deal. Knowing that you are always calm will help sooth your clients and increase their confidence in you.

Here are just a few of the common issues that can lead to anger on the part of clients:

- The loan appraisal comes in below the purchase price, angering both buyer and seller.
- There is a significant delay on the part of the lender in getting the loan approved.
- The seller fails to perform as required in the contract.
- The buyer fails to perform as required in the contract.
- An inspector is unable to do a crucial inspection for several weeks.
- The buyer's offer is rejected by the seller.
- The seller leaves a great deal of trash and debris for the buyer to clean up.
- The seller fails to leave personal property that was promised in the contract.

- The seller leaves personal property as stipulated in the contract but it is broken.
- The listing has been sitting on the market for several weeks with no offers.
- A pest control inspection reveals significantly more damage than anyone anticipated.
- A roof report finds that the roof must be totally removed and replaced.

You can see why I contend that we are problem solvers, not salespeople. In frustrating situations, anger can be defused using specific techniques. Let's use an owner whose listing has expired as an example, because these folks are notorious for being angry and difficult to deal with.

When a listing expires, the home owner is usually angry because he has been inconvenienced with absolutely no reward at the end of several months. He might have stored some of his favorite pieces of furniture somewhere else and had to keep the property in perfect condition every single day. During the time his listing was active, some agents had probably called for an appointment and then didn't show up. It's also likely that some agents showed up without calling in advance.

The main reason the house didn't sell was probably because it was overpriced. However, because an agent took the listing at that price, it implied that the house really would sell for that amount and, as a result, the owner probably felt that his agent and the entire real estate profession let him down. Frankly, it's not only frustrating but also embarrassing for friends and family to know that you had your house on the market and it failed to sell.

As a result of these and other factors, most home owners whose listings have expired are angry. One of the reasons agents are reluctant to work with expired listings is because they don't want to face this anger or they don't know how to defuse it.

Actually, it's not that difficult to deflect anger. People who deal with anger for a living, such as mental health professionals and hostage negotiators, all follow the same basic system, which can work for real estate professionals as well.

The first rule is to let the seller vent his anger. You should take notes as he does because they will form the basis of your listing presentation. This at least makes him feel that somebody cares, and for a lot of people, that's enough. Then they can move on.

However, the real secret to defusing anger is to encourage the seller to keep venting until he has totally exhausted his list of complaints. Until he feels fully heard, he will not be ready to listen to anything you have to say.

Once he has "run out of gas," you can use your list to address all his areas of unhappiness. This list is powerful because the owner has just given you a customized listing presentation. You do not have to do everything on the list, but you should at least address each item. This shows that you have been listening and are concerned about his needs.

Again, the same technique can be used with any upset client. First, listen to her complaints. Second, encourage her to keep talking. Third, take notes about why she is upset. Fourth, when she has no more complaints, begin addressing her issues one at a time. Above all, just listen.

84) BE STRATEGIC—NOT TRANSACTION-ORIENTED

Wouldn't it be nice to be able to completely stop your marketing and just concentrate on your clients? While it may sound far-fetched, it is possible if you build client relationships for a lifetime. This way, as your young clients go from owning a starter home or condominium, to all of their upgrades in homes throughout the years, you will be there to help them. Not only will they have a trusted friend to turn to whenever it's time to sell and buy a new home, but you will already know their needs because of your history with them.

Unfortunately, most salespeople in America rarely see the same customers twice, and that's a shame because repeat clients reduce your marketing efforts and just make sales more fun. I have had some of the same clients for over 30 years and have helped them buy small starter homes, trade up to median priced properties, and then purchase some of the nicest homes in my area. Having a regular base of customers you can count on year after year helps give you achieve longevity in a very difficult business like real estate.

The first couple of years in real estate are the most difficult because you do not have any clients and you must start building your business from scratch. After two or three years, however, you should have a small base of clients to build on, and eventually these clients will start to buy and sell more property as well as provide you with referrals.

If you stay in touch with your clients, they can give you business throughout your life, and eventually provide you with a valuable database that you can sell whenever you decide to retire from the real estate profession. As has been mentioned over and over, you must stay in touch with your clients.

Too many agents take a very shortsighted view of our business, so they go from transaction to transaction rather than building a business (see Tip #111). The problem with this philosophy is that on January first of each year, you must start all over again looking for business. All that marketing takes time and money. Whereas if you had an ever-expanding base of clients that you built up over time, this would almost certainly guarantee a minimum number of transactions a year because circumstances dictate that a percentage of the population will always have to move for various reasons. With a steady block of business virtually assured each year, your marketing efforts would only be needed to add additional profit to your business—not for survival.

I can also tell you that it's extremely gratifying to watch clients progress up the ladder of real estate ownership and even into real estate investing. Their success is your success.

85) EFFICIENTLY SHOW PROPERTIES TO BUYERS

Buyers hire agents to save them time in the home buying process. Nothing sells your value more than being efficient in showing properties. This part of the process can be a huge waste of time if you don't know what you're doing or where you're going.

By "efficient," I don't necessarily mean you always have to take the shortest route to the property. Obviously, you don't want to wander all over town for no reason, but remember that people buy neighborhoods first, then homes. Don't be afraid to tell them you're taking the "scenic route" to the house. (I say to "tell them" because the last thing you want to do on the way to a property is get lost. You can't expect them to believe you are the expert on the area if you get lost.) Be sure to drive by all the amenities so they can see that it's a great place to live. Include parks, golf courses, freeway access, shopping centers, and any place else that is a real sales point.

Also, don't show properties the way average agents do. They usually save the best house for last, thinking clients will appreciate a house more after they have seen a few lemons. Unfortunately, all this does is build unrealistic expectations in clients' minds because they are led to believe that every house they see will be better than the last. After seeing the last house, they still expect to see one that is markedly better. Don't do this to your clients or to yourself! Instead, always show the house you think will best meet your client's needs, followed by one that doesn't compare as well. The house that suits him best will give him a good perspective from which to view everything that follows. It usually causes him to want to go back for a second look after visiting the disappointing homes.

This technique will help your clients come to a decision more quickly, saving them time and reducing confusion.

86) PRESENT OFFERS FOR MAXIMUM EFFECTIVENESS

When a buyer actually decides to bid on a house, the fingernail biting begins. As the minutes tick by, he becomes more and more invested in the deal going through. He tries to guess at what the other offers will be and ticks off the reasons in his head as to why they'll be unacceptable to the seller. Some people mentally move into the house during this period and start hanging paintings on the walls. After all that, he doesn't want to hear that he was rejected.

So make sure that doesn't happen any more often than it has to. The way you present offers has a lot to do with whether they're accepted. It can either help or hurt your buyer's chances. There are several ways to bump up your offer.

First, you want to write as clean an offer as possible. In order to do that, you have to call the listing agent before you sit down with your clients to write it. You shouldn't call the agent after you've written the offer because, ethically, once you have written one, you have to disclose it. And that can present a problem, because certain unscrupulous listing agents use that offer to encourage other agents in their own office to get their clients to also submit offers on the same property before it's too late. (After all, the agent's commission is often higher if he sells a house to another agent within his own company.) These new offers could then beat out yours.

It's also to your advantage to find out if other offers are coming in, so ask the listing agent. If there are others, it could affect the purchase agreement that you write—you might just want to send in your best offer straight away, rather than starting low. In addition, try to discover whether the seller has any preferences or requirements that you should be informed about and why he put the house on the market in the first place. While the listing agent is not required to answer any of your questions, he might throw you a tidbit or two, and any information he provides will increase the chances of your offer being accepted.

Second, try to present your offer in person to both the listing agent and the seller. No one can sell your clients and their proposal like you can. It also gives you the opportunity to observe facial expressions and other nuances that you wouldn't be privy to on the phone.

Third, when you do have the opportunity to present your offer in person, never bring out the contract until you first have a little time to build a rapport with the listing agent and seller. Compliment the seller on her house and explain a little about your buyers. I may bring out a few photos and even a handwritten letter from the buyers saying how much they like the house. These can be especially effective in multiple-offer situations where I've managed to make the sellers feel an emotional attachment to my buyer. In some cases, my buyers have gotten the property even though they did not present the highest price.

Next, ask the listing agent and seller to allow you to wait as they discuss your client's offer. I usually say something like, "If you feel the need to write a counteroffer, please don't do so before bringing me back in to talk about it. There's no point in killing any more trees than necessary." Most of the time I'm allowed to do this, and I use it as an opportunity to renegotiate with the seller before they write a counter. I do this because I only want to leave with one of two counteroffers—preferably one that is acceptable to my clients (who may be waiting outside in the car to acknowledge a ratified contract or sign a counter), or one that is totally unacceptable so we don't waste any more time.

This system will greatly increase the chances of your clients being able to buy the home of their dreams.

BUSINESS PRACTICES

87) LET THEM KNOW YOU'RE A SERIOUS PROFESSIONAL

In America especially, presentation is everything. You can't expect people to take you seriously if you're dressed for play. When you step into a meeting with someone who is trusting you with hundreds of thousands of dollars of their hard-earned money, you need to broadcast that you are the consummate professional. This is probably more important for real estate agents than others because our image has become rather tarnished over the years.

First impressions are critical. I know we've all heard the expression "Don't judge a book by its cover," but if this were true, if people didn't do it, why would publishers spend a fortune every year designing book covers? Every time you are out in public, you are marketing a product—you. What do you want your apparel to say about you?

Dressing professionally sells your value to clients. If you've ever bought expensive software for your computer you'll notice it comes in a large box, but the product is actually only a CD-ROM about the size of a small pancake. Since the CD-ROM only costs a few dollars, why did the company spend so much money for packaging? Well, would you pay $200 for something that is the size of a CD if it didn't look a lot bigger and fancier? This is why it comes in a big ornate box.

In the same way, if you want to charge a high fee for your services, you must look like an expensive product. This is not to say that you also don't deliver value, but remember those first impressions.

The good news is that it doesn't take a lot of effort to stand out from the crowd of average agents. One of the quickest ways to differentiate yourself is to dress professionally all the time. Some agents show up in baseball caps thinking they're putting their clients at ease, but all it does is tell them that this person isn't taking them or their business seriously.

I'm not saying you always have to wear a suit because in some locations, such as resort areas, this might look ridiculous. However, to dress professionally in any situation, just follow this one rule of thumb: Be a bit more formal than your client. For example, if your clients wear dress shirts or blouses, you should wear a business suit. If they wear polo shirts, then wear a polo shirt with a blazer over it. If the women are wearing flats, you should wear heels.

You might even consider hiring a wardrobe consultant to help you select the best clothes for your body type, skin tone, and hair color. Believe it or not, these are all factors that affect how different cuts and colors of clothing look on you. The right clothes can make you appear trimmer, healthier, and more confident.

While there are always exceptions to every rule, here are just a couple of suggestions for real estate professionals:

- **Clean shoes.** We often spend a lot of time and money making sure our clothes are clean and then neglect our shoes. Just make sure they're clean—unless you are working for a builder, where a bit of mud on the soles could be a sign of respect.
- **Polished shoes.** If you wear shoes that can be polished, have them shined regularly.

- **Well-groomed hairstyle.** If you've been going to the same hair-cutter or stylist for the past 20 or 30 years, it might be time to update your hairstyle so you look like a person of your times. If you're selling real estate in the 21st century, don't look like you're stuck in the 1950s.
- **Cleaned and trimmed fingernails.** This is one of the most over-looked areas of hygiene, and yet speaks volumes about you. No matter how much money you spend on clothing, if you have dirty fingernails, you might as well have shopped at a thrift store.
- **Minimal perfume or cologne.** Many people today are very sensitive to scents and some can even become sick breathing them. This is why hospitals forbid patients and staff from wearing any kind of perfume or cologne. If you wear these scents in your off-hours, give them the "sniff test" before spraying them on for work. If people can detect it from more than three feet away, you're wearing too much.
- **Brushed teeth and fresh breath.** With all the gum and breath fresheners available, there is no excuse for "morning breath" at any time of the day or night. Remember that real estate is a very personal business; we're in close proximity to our clients for long periods of time. There's nothing worse than having to breathe through your mouth for hours to avoid someone else's bad breath!
- **Use deodorant regularly.** What more do I need to say about this? Use it but use it sparingly, because it's not a substitute for regular baths or showers.
- **Body piercing.** I'll leave this up to your own discretion. Many clients expect to be working with a rather conservative person, so it's probably not appropriate. Something about a brass ring through the nose doesn't scream "professional." However, if most of your clients have various types of body piercings, then go for it!

Remember, in our business we're always on stage. I've had agents show up to a real estate class in shorts and torn T-shirts. Sure, their attire shouldn't affect their ability to gain insights from the course, but do you think other agents will trust them with referrals? It's okay to be casual but you can still look professional.

88) WEAR A NAME BADGE OR CAREER APPAREL

Did you ever walk into a large retail store looking for help and you couldn't tell the employees from the customers? Or worse yet, the patrons looked more professional than the workers?

Displaying a name badge with your company name and logo is an easy way to let people know that you are a real estate professional. In fact, you are more likely to drum up business at the grocery store and the bank wearing your badge than sitting in your office waiting for clients to fall into your lap.

I know agents that really do get business at the grocery store, the bank, the stationery store, the sandwich shop, and elsewhere just because they are wearing their badge. Once, a bank teller called me to the front of the line to meet a couple who had recently moved to the area and were looking to buy a home. This all happened because the teller knew I was in real estate—just from my badge.

Even more effective than wearing a badge is wearing *career apparel*—clothing that has either the REALTOR® "R" symbol or the name of your company permanently embroidered on it. In addition to being a great marketing tool, this also makes the clothing tax deductible because it's a walking advertisement—although a little classier than a sandwich board. Clothing is more effective than name badges because you can wear it anywhere that logo clothing is customarily worn, such as on picnics, hiking and biking trails, and on the golfing green.

My experience owning and managing many real estate offices where I required our agents to wear career apparel every day was that it added to their sales by two to four extra transactions a year. Because the clothes get people to come to you, you aren't in the position of having to chase down clients, which makes you look like a pushy salesperson, not a helpful consultant.

For example, one afternoon I was at the post office wearing a tie with a very small REALTOR® logo embroidered on it. The clerk behind the counter recognized the logo and asked me to look at his mother's house, which I then listed. On another occasion, I was at a party wearing a polo shirt with my real estate company name in the same place where others were wearing logos like Izod. In under 90 minutes, three people had come up to me and asked me to help them buy and sell real estate without me mentioning the word once.

Women agents often complain about the lack of choices in female career apparel. If this is the case, just look for a shop than can embroider the REALTOR® logo or your company name on clothing. This way you can customize clothes that you would wear anyway. You don't have to wear something unstylish just because it has a logo. Now you have no excuse for not donning career apparel every day.

Career apparel can also simplify your life and help you be more time efficient. If you have several white logo shirts or blouses, you can wear them with almost anything. The selection process is cut down to five minutes. Have dress shirts for winter and polo shirts for summer. Have long-sleeve and short-sleeve and a variety of colors. You can coordinate your outfits so well that you could get dressed in the dark and still look like a topflight professional.

Wearing career apparel or a badge lets people know you're a real estate professional. When they are in need of an agent, you'll already be imprinted in their subconscious minds through the power of repeated impressions.

89) HAVE EVERY BUYER SIGN A BUYER-BROKER AGREEMENT

In some parts of the country, having buyers sign a Buyer-Broker Agreement is standard practice, but in many areas it's rare. Sure, there are many benefits to the agent of having potential buyers sign a Buyer-Broker Agreement. However, there are also tremendous benefits to the buyer to make an exclusive commitment to one agent. Besides, if there were nothing in it for buyers to sign a Buyer-Broker Agreement, they would never sign it.

So what are the benefits to the client of signing a Buyer-Broker Agreement? We must explain to buyers that this contract enables us to show them all the properties that are on the market in their price range and in the area they want to buy. It's a little-known fact that without this agreement, most agents will hide properties from clients. Why? Because they won't get paid!

For instance, most agents won't show for-sale-by-owners' properties to buyers unless they have a signed Buyer-Broker Agreement. Without it, if the seller takes your client aside and suggests he come back later without you and they strike a deal, you are entitled to absolutely nothing. This is because you have no employment agreement with either the buyer or seller to pay you for your work. A Buyer-Broker Agreement would generally have the buyer pay the commission if the seller does not.

Another type of property that some agents avoid showing without a Buyer-Broker Agreement is new homes. Many builders do not offer any compensation or only a reduced commission to real estate agents because they have their own internal sales staff to pay as well. Again, the Buyer-Broker Agreement would make the buyer responsible for compensating his broker.

Yet another situation where agents may be reluctant to show properties in the absence of a Buyer-Broker Agreement is those paying a lower commission than they would like. Instead, they will show the higher commission houses. With a Buyer-Broker agreement, the buyer makes up the difference between what the seller is offering and what the broker and client have agreed upon.

Those were the advantages to you of having this agreement with a buyer. There are benefits to them as well. For instance, if the seller is offering additional compensation to the agent representing the buyer, such as $1,000 or a trip to Hawaii, in the absence of any other agreement this automatically goes to the selling broker. Under a Buyer-Broker Agreement, however, the parties could agree to split the additional incentive, give it all to the buyer, or anything else the parties desire.

The Buyer-Broker Agreement is like a listing agreement with a seller. It is an employment agreement that promises that the buyer will pay you a commission if she buys any property through anyone during your listing period.

Would you ever work a listing without a signed listing agreement? Who is more likely to waste your time—a buyer or a seller? So why would you ever work with a buyer without having them sign a Buyer-Broker Agreement?

Just because others in your area do not use this valuable document does not mean that you shouldn't. If you do what average agents do, you will get what average agents get—an average income.

Not only does it assure the buyer's loyalty to you, but it also assures him that you will show him every property on the market that he is qualified to buy. Without it, most agents will not show for-sale-by-owner properties, lower commission listings, new homes where the builder is not cooperating, and more. Again this is because there is no assurance they will get paid or compensated to the level they are comfortable.

Studies show that buyers want to have their own agent and are willing to pay for him or her. While the seller usually compensates the agent who represents the buyer, there is always the possibility that the buyer will have to do so. Buyers should also understand that if they buy through someone else after signing a Buyer-Broker Agreement with you, they will owe *two* commissions.

Signing the Buyer-Broker Agreement is the ultimate test of loyalty for buyers. If you clearly explain all the benefits and responsibilities of the contract and they won't sign it, this most likely means they do not intend to be loyal to you. When would you want to find this out? At the beginning of your relationship or six months later after you have shown them a hundred houses?

If you practice in an area where buyer brokerage is not widely used, you will need to attend a seminar or buy a CD about how to sell the agreement to potential clients. While there can be benefits to the broker as well as the buyer, you will want to learn a step-by-step presentation for explaining the benefits to buyers just as you would do for sellers.

It's usually best to explain the Buyer-Broker Agreement to potential clients before you ever show them property. This way you can determine if they are going to be loyal to you before you create an agency relationship with them.

90) PRICE YOUR LISTINGS TO SELL

Properties for sale that are priced properly generally sell quickly and even generate multiple offers. However, not all sellers are willing to put a realistic price tag on their homes.

If you had a friend who wanted to sell a used book on eBay, would there be any point in telling him to price it at twice what a new book would sell for? Would you tell someone to charge three times the going rate for garden work? The asking price—no matter how giddy it makes the seller feel—is beside the point if no one will pay it. The same is true of houses. You are not serving your clients if you give in to their grandiosity and let them ask for an absurd amount for a house, when you know it will never sell at that price. Six months down the line, it will still be sitting there, and it is quite dispiriting to have to keep knocking thousands of dollars off the listing amount until some buyer finally bites. Even if the final price is fairly reasonable, the seller ends up feeling he only got a bargain basement deal, and the property looks tainted because it didn't sell.

Whether it's a buyers' or a sellers' market, you want to price your listings so they sell. Nobody wins if they just sit on the market. Agents certainly try to be reasonable, but sometimes clients insist that they "try it a little higher for a while to test the market." There is a problem with this tactic. If it doesn't sell within three to four weeks, whether or not the seller reduces the price, it is now "stale." Anyone who has previously seen the property now believes that the seller is not serious or motivated, and any offers that come in will be low.

Particularly in a buyers' market, you've got to be very firm with your sellers about the price range in which their property is most likely to sell. If they want to list at a price that is higher than your competitive market analysis (CMA) shows, explain to them that "the sales price of a property must be justified to three people. First, to agents, otherwise they won't bring their buyers to look at your house. Second, to buyers, or they won't make an offer that gets accepted. Third, to bank appraisers, or they won't be able to convince the lender to give the buyer enough of a loan to buy the property. Then show them the comparables on your CMA and ask, "Which comps should I use to justify your price?" Hopefully this will show them that even if their house did sell for more than your CMA can currently justify, the buyer wouldn't be able to purchase the home anyway because they won't get enough of a loan.

As I said, the last thing you want is for a property to be *tainted*. This term usually applies to places where some notorious event has taken place—for instance, a mass murder that occurred in the house—so the place is now associated with something horrific. Yet it can also be applied to properties that have languished on the market.

By the time the seller lists the property with another broker at a lower price, most of the local agents and buyers have already lost interest and the seller has an albatross on his hands. The only way to rekindle interest is to upgrade the property in some way. Typically, people will radically drop the price, change the whole look with some outstanding landscaping, or add new features. Some people take the property off the market for a few weeks and then bring it back on as if it were a new listing, although the ethics of this move is often disputed, and it rarely does any good.

All the machinations agents go through to rekindle interest in properties that are stale just emphasizes how important it is to not overprice it in the first place. People don't go out searching for the biggest purchase of their lives without doing their homework first. Even if they aren't working with an agent, they pretty much know how much they have to cough up for a particular property, and the seller isn't going to pull the wool over their eyes.

If you have a seller who thinks you should price his property above what other buyers are paying for similar properties (unless it's a rapidly appreciating market), suggest that she list it with another agent as a two-week listing to see if somebody else can sell it for that outrageous price. (Don't do it yourself because you don't want an expired listing on your record.) Make sure the new agent lists at the unrealistic price the client is insisting she can get. What will probably happen is that the property will fail to sell, and the new agent will just try to get the seller to lower the price. At this point, the client will probably come back to you because the other agent lied to her. It is obvious that he was only trying to get her listing, whereas you are the one who told her the truth.

Price your listings to sell or walk away from the listing. It is better to spend your time marketing a few saleable listings than waste your time with several overpriced properties.

91) EDUCATE SELLERS ABOUT THE VALUE OF THE "FOR SALE" SIGN

Some sellers won't allow a "For Sale" sign on their property because they "don't want their neighbors to know their house is on the market." They're afraid that leaving will be seen as abandoning their neighbors, or they don't want nosy neighbors to know their business. In actuality, you as the agent want the neighbors to know because their word of mouth creates more visitors on open house day; they often have friends who want to move into the neighborhood. Sellers may also believe that a sign only helps the broker, not the seller.

We must educate them for their own best interests that, yes, they *do* want a "For Sale" sign on the house. Without a sign, all their neighbors who have friends or relatives who would like to live in the neighborhood won't know about its availability. Also, those same neighbors are going to know something is up when strange cars start parking in front at all times of the day and night. I jokingly tell my clients, "As a result of all the traffic my marketing will generate, without a sign your neighbors might think you've become a drug dealer!" They usually get the point and let me put a sign up.

We must also explain to our clients that, while a sign may not directly generate a buyer for any one specific property, it helps the marketing with all of our listings. In other words, buyers who call our office because they have seen a sign on one house may not be interested in that house but can be referred to yours and vice versa.

The easiest way to get sellers to allow you to put a "For Sale" sign on their property is first, to tell them the advantages in general, and second, to quantify what it will cost them to not have one. For instance, I usually tell sellers that I believe not having the sign will reduce their eventual sales price by about five percent. This, straight off, is due to the loss of buyers that the neighbors might present. So, if their house is normally worth $300,000 when using all the regular marketing techniques, the lack of a sign makes the house worth only $285,000. That is a real eye-opener! Then I go on to tell sellers that we might as well lower the price now. When they can visibly see the loss in value because there's no sign, they usually just say, "Where do you want it, in the window or on the lawn?" Argument over.

92) EDUCATE SELLERS ABOUT THE VALUE OF HAVING A LOCK BOX

Some sellers balk at the idea of having a real estate lock box with the keys to their house on their front door. They sometimes worry about safety and privacy. Explain to them about all the security features of the modern electronic lock box and be sure there is a separate dead bolt for privacy.

If they still resist, you can use the same tactic and a similar argument as the "For Sale" sign. Explain to the seller that many agents will not drive to your office to pick up a key. They're not going to drive their buyers all the way across town just to show the listing and then drive back to return the key. Sellers easily accept it when I tell them that 10 percent of agents will probably decide not to include their house on the list that they're showing their clients if they have to do that. If their house would normally be worth $300,000, it is now only worth $270,000 just because of reduced showings. Again, the discussion is ended at this point. They usually say to me, "Where do you want the lock box, on the door or the water pipe?"

When you quantify what the person's resistance to fully marketing the property is costing her, you are using a powerful tool indeed. This illustration convinces the seller to do what is in her own best interests. Once she can compare the flimsiness of her objections to the dollar amount she is flushing away, it is almost impossible not to capitulate and do what is necessary. Boiling an argument down to dollars and cents is the quickest way to change a mind.

93) LEARN TO CLOSE YOUR CLIENTS

Human nature is a tough nut to crack. If you give people the choice to do what they need so they can get what they want, in contrast with the choice to do absolutely nothing, the human tendency is to do nothing. Why? Because it's safer not to make a decision. The problem is that when someone is not making a decision, they actually are making one—they just don't know it. Unfortunately, they are deciding to not get what they want because they won't act.

Agents possess the same strange aspect of human nature. They know that the practice of closing techniques is an art that must be learned. They can simply take a class or buy a book on closing techniques. Yet so many agents skip this vital step.

Once we have spent time asking questions and talking to our clients over a period of time, we know that either buying or selling a house is a decision they really do want to make. And we know that it is in their best interests to launch into this venture full speed ahead. However, they have a lot of fear about doing it, and we must help them.

Signing a contract means making a decision and decisions in and of themselves are a bit scary. Even worse, you are making a commitment and you could make a mistake, and then you can't take your signature back.

Here are some popular closing techniques that will help clients do what they have to do so they can have what they want:

- **The assumptive close:** Just proceed as if your client has already made a decision. To buyers you can ask, "Would you want to move in within 30 or 60 days?" To sellers you can ask, "Do you want the 'For Sale' sign on the lawn or in the window?" You don't care which answer they give, as long as it isn't no. These questions make the process move forward because they are precisely what you would ask if the client had already committed.

- **The Ben Franklin close:** According to legend, Ben Franklin would use this technique to decide on whether he would go ahead with a new project or not. He simply drew a line down the middle of a piece of paper and put the benefits (pros) on the left side and the drawbacks (cons) on the right. Whichever list was longer guided his decision. You can use this technique with sellers when they're trying to decide if they should sell now, or buyers when they're trying to decide between one house and another.

- **The feel-felt-found close:** There is a magical phrase you can use that's called "feel, felt, found." Almost immediately it shows that you have empathy for the quagmire they feel they're in. When you show that you know how they feel, you help clients overcome their reluctance. It has a way of quieting their fears and making it easy to move on, in spite of the fear. For buyers who are afraid they can't afford the mortgage payments, you can respond, "I know how you feel because I felt the same way when I bought my last house. What I found is that while the payments may seem high at first, you will learn to budget for them the same way you do for all your other expenses. After a while, you won't even notice them." For sellers who aren't sure they should accept the first offer (everyone thinks the big spender hasn't walked through their door yet), you can respond, "I know how you feel because I felt the same way when I sold my house. What I found is there is always the possibility of another offer eventually coming in. But the first couple of offers are usually the most serious and the most likely to close."

If you do take a class in closing techniques, you will learn many others besides the ones listed above. No matter which one you choose though, you must remember your central task: help your clients come to the decision they really need to make. You're not forcing them to do anything that isn't in their best interests. In a sense, you are like a tennis coach giving his star pupil pointers on how to win the game. Perhaps she doesn't want to change her game or she is going through some inertia and doesn't want to practice at all. But the coach knows that deep down, all she wants to do is win.

94) CONSIDER BEING THE LAST AGENT TO PRESENT TO SELLERS

Aren't sellers entitled to the best listing agent available—you? Shouldn't the decision be easy for them to make? By being the last agent to conduct your listing presentation you can accomplish both of these goals.

I'm sure there are readers who like to be the first agent to conduct their listing presentation to a seller. I like to be the last agent to present because I am so sick and tired of being told, "Michael, we really liked you and your presentation. However, we've promised two more agents that we would interview them. It's only fair to give them the same courtesy as we've given you. But I'm sure we'll be calling you back." They don't. I doubt that they even remember me by the end of the day. If, on the other hand, I am the last one they see, they cannot use this argument.

Now you're probably thinking, "What if an aggressive agent who is ahead of you pushes the seller to sign with them?" That would be fine with me. You have to understand my system to understand why it's fine with me. I ask the seller if I can be the last agent to present during our very first conversation. They expect a reason, so I tell them, "I have unique marketing techniques that you can't appreciate until you see what other agents *don't* have." This gets their curiosity up so they can't wait to hear what they are. How are the techniques different? I give them a targeted marketing program as outlined in Tip #75. At the end of this conversation, I ask them not to sign anything with anyone else until we've had a chance to meet.

Next, remember I meet with sellers before they *begin* their interviews with the first agent. At that time I give them the list of questions to ask all of us agents, and I give them a letter reconfirming our appointment after all of the other agents have done their presentations. Again, it reminds them not to sign with anyone yet.

Think about it. They promised me over the phone and in writing that they would not list with anyone until we've met. If they sign with another agent, they are liars and that agent is welcome to them. If they will lie at the beginning of this relationship, how do you think they will handle disclosures like the Transfer Disclosure Statement?

Be the last agent to present and never leave without the listing.

95) OFFER A GUARANTEE TO BUYERS

Like sellers, buyers can be reluctant to make a commitment to an agent they have met for the first time. Signing a Buyer-Broker Agreement can be a bit imposing.

This is why it's crucial to have a logical, step-by-step presentation for buyers just like I'm sure you have a listing presentation for sellers. I always ask potential buyers to come into the office to sit down for about an hour. Some buyers who are not used to a listing presentation may balk at first, but when you explain that there are benefits for them to do so, the serious ones will do it.

As always, I start out every presentation—whether for buyers, sellers, FSBOs, or expired listings—the exact same way, by explaining how I earn my money and how little agents really make. For buyers I then explain all the benefits of the Buyer-Broker Agreement (see Tip #89).

Whenever I get the objection "We want to think about it," I simply say, "I offer a guarantee that if you are unhappy with my services you can cancel the Buyer-Broker Agreement at any time. So, now what is there to think about?" At this point serious buyers will usually sign the contract because they know they could always back out.

Now, I know what you're thinking: "What if I find them a home they really like? What keeps them from canceling our agreement and then either buying through another agent or directly from the seller so they don't have to pay me a commission?" During my buyer presentation, I explain that if they decide to cancel my agreement, the broker protection clause still applies. In other words, if they buy any property I have shown them, they must wait a minimum length of time before purchasing it. I generally use a six-month listing period because, since I'm offering a guarantee, what would be the harm in signing? This also becomes the length of the protection clause.

Yes, they can still buy the house I showed them six months after canceling our agreement. However, what kind of deal would it be if it were still on the market after six months? Frankly, this has never happened to me. Once clients understand and sign the Buyer-Broker Agreement, they generally live up to the terms.

96) DEVELOP GOOD RELATIONS WITH PROPERTY APPRAISERS

Developing and maintaining good working relations with appraisers can benefit both your sellers and buyers. They are not your enemy as some agents would have you believe.

Your seller might do everything she is supposed to do, yet still run into trouble because an appraiser can't find comparable properties to bring the appraisal in at the sales price of the property. This, of course, lowers the amount of the loan the lender will provide. The buyer might be a well-qualified borrower, but if the property itself doesn't qualify for the asking price, she will have to come up with a larger down payment, which she may not have.

A good appraiser should be an asset to your seller, and you can help make that a reality. Develop positive relationships with them at all times because it will go a long way toward making transactions go much more smoothly. Appraisers can make or break your deal simply by the way they approach the appraisal of your property. They can be creative in finding comparable properties outside your area so they can appraise the property for the sales price. Or, they can be conservative and stick to the guidelines, and then the buyer cannot get the loan he needs.

If you are on friendly terms with the appraiser, you might get him to ask for your assistance. For instance, I once sold a house for $250,000 more than any other similar property had sold for in history. I was able to do this with clever marketing and staging of the property, which generated 18 offers on the house. I then needed the appraiser to sign off on it. Fortunately, I knew the man so he called me to ask how I thought he could justify our sales price to the lender. I convinced him by pointing out that we had 17 other buyers willing to pay close to this price, thus proving that it must be worth that price. According to an appraiser's definition, value is what a buyer is willing to pay. In addition, the appraiser knows that if this buyer defaults, any of the other 17 will step forward to buy the property for the same price.

Good relations with an appraiser can make or break a deal. So how do you develop good relations with them? Simple—be responsive and helpful. If one calls you for information about one of your past sales, return the call immediately. Many agents don't want to bother because the call is about a deal that is already closed; they're only concerned about the next one. The appraiser, however, needs information on this sale and is asking for your help. Don't be short-sighted. Remember that the appraiser you help today could be in a position to help you tomorrow.

Many real estate agents fear appraisers because in the past, they made a loan difficult. Remember, it's in the bank's best interests to approve a loan for your client. Do what you can to make their job easier. If you know of sales of comparable properties that they might consider, be sure to offer these to them. They might be a little outside the area but similar enough to be used by a lender.

97) OFFER STAGING CONSULTATION

Effective staging can help a house sell faster and make the decision to buy easier for purchasers. *Staging* a property, or hiring a pro to do it for you, is one of the most important things you can do, not only to sell a client's house, but to sell it faster and get the best possible price for it. You're not deceiving anyone. All you are doing is showing off the product in the most positive light. It's just like a fashion show on a runway. Designers *could* drape their clothes on someone who is overweight and out of shape, but what value would that add to the clothes? They want thin, beautiful women to make that tiny bikini look like it should cost $480. When you bring in leather couches, Persian carpets, and Greek vases, and you arrange them so the rooms look luxurious and comfortable, you make a world of difference in how a property shows. It gives the potential buyer the best impression from the very beginning.

However, you must learn the art of staging because most of us are not graced with good fashion sense. You may want to hire a professional stager, especially for larger or more expensive properties. Even if you do that, it is still good for you to learn the basics of staging so you can not only help clients do minor staging themselves, but also because it will help you recognize when it's time to hire a professional stager on particularly difficult properties.

Knowing about staging adds value to your services. Even small changes can make a big difference in how buyers perceive the property. Start with inexpensive steps such as uncluttering, adding accessories, and cleaning. Virtually any house will look better with these kinds of embellishments. The use of different colors, textures, patterns, and accent pieces can make small rooms appear larger and cold rooms feel warmer. Effective staging cannot change a house, but it does enhance its positive aspects and deemphasize any of its negative aspects.

Probably the most difficult task when it comes to staging has to do with how to tell the owner that her house needs a lot of help. Many people these days see themselves as amateur interior designers, and they think the heart-print wallpaper that matches perfectly with the pink sofa is stunning. So step one is to do it as diplomatically as you possibly can. Let a professional stager help you because communicating with the owner is part of her job.

Remember, the rule of thumb is to present a house in such a way that anyone looking at it can see how his or her own taste would apply. You don't want anyone to walk away because the decorating is so overwhelming that they can't picture themselves in this home. Here are a few basic tips that will make any house show better:

Inside the House

1. Remove all unnecessary items of furniture such as overstuffed easy chairs, large couches, and extra leaves in dining tables. This will make the house seem larger and less cluttered.
2. Unclutter the house further by storing small knickknacks, like statues and collectibles, out of sight.
3. Keep the kitchen counters clear of anything but usable cooking items.
4. Remove any unneeded items from the bathroom including the scale and toilet brush; they make an already small room seem even more claustrophobic.
5. Minimize the number of pictures on the walls. Remember, as much as possible—blank slate.

Outside the House

1. Clean up everything from outside the house including garbage cans, woodpiles, and other obstructions.
2. Trim all trees, plants, and bushes away from the house.
3. Consider having the outside professionally landscaped. It can make your house look like it is surrounded by a garden.
4. Make sure the paint is in good condition, especially the trim and gutters.

Look at both the inside and outside of the house from the buyers' perspective. It must be inviting and welcoming as a first impression. Otherwise, have the owner fix it.

98) SOLVE CLIENTS' PROBLEMS

People want to buy and sell real estate in order to solve some problem in their lives. Buyers might want to reduce their taxes, build equity for future investment or retirement, make sure that a landlord cannot raise their rent, or a dozen other reasons. Sellers may want to sell so they can cash in on their equity, relocate to another city, divorce their spouse, move to a larger house, downsize to a smaller home, or move closer to family members. There's an old saying that "If you want to develop the right solution, you must first correctly diagnose the problem." Your job is to find out what their problem is so you can solve it. So you have to determine why they want to buy or sell because each problem requires a different solution.

The best way to find the problem is to ask effective questions. Probe for meaning and do not be satisfied with superficial answers. The reason a seller wants to sell could impact her listing price and the price she might accept. For example, if you discover that a couple is going through a very rancorous divorce and their house is the last thing they own together, they might want you to list it at the lower end of the value range just to get rid of it—so they can be rid of each other. If you have buyers who badly need write-offs on their taxes, they may be less concerned about the price they pay and more interested in the deductions it will generate. But you won't know about any of this if you don't get to know your clients.

You also have to find out the depth of the problem. In other words, how serious is it? The more serious his challenge, the more motivated he is to buy or sell. However, if you discover through your inquiries that there is no problem the client is trying to solve, or it's a rather minor one, he is unlikely to be strongly motivated and you know what that means. He probably will resist doing everything you tell him to do. The way it works is that the more pressing the challenge he is facing, the more motivated he will be.

99) PRESENT YOUR OFFERS IN PERSON WHENEVER POSSIBLE

When you have an offer to present for a buyer, the chances of getting a ratified contract increase dramatically when you present your offer in person. No one can present the case for the seller to accept your offer better than you can, especially when you find yourself in a multiple-offer situation.

Now I know that in many regions of the country, allowing the selling agent to present his or her offer in person is not a common practice. Who cares? Just because it isn't regularly done doesn't mean it can't be done at all. Try asking, because all they can do is say no.

Here's the reason why I try to present all my offers in person. During my presentation, I will build a rapport with the seller and try to find out as much as I can about the facts and circumstances surrounding the sale of his property. Is he in a hurry to sell? Is he buying or building another house? Don't ever bring out your offer until you've built a rapport, otherwise the seller will focus on it and not you.

After presenting the offer, I will say something to the listing agent like, "I know you recognize that this is an excellent offer from a very qualified buyer. If, for some reason, you feel compelled to give us a counteroffer, please don't write anything up without us first discussing it. That will save you time and keep us from killing any more trees. Please take your time discussing our offer, and I'll be out in my car waiting."

What happens when they bring me back in is that I basically now renegotiate the whole deal right there, using the knowledge I had gained earlier and what they tell me they are thinking about as a counteroffer.

The whole goal for presenting offers in person is that you only want to leave the seller's house with one of three things: the best would be a ratified purchase agreement with no counteroffer; second best is a counteroffer you know your buyer will accept; and last, a rejected offer. The one thing you do not want to do is go back and forth between the seller and buyer over rather minor points that could have been resolved much earlier.

There are several reasons why listing agents should want you to present your own offer in person. First is that there is liability on their part if they refuse to let buyers' agents present offers on behalf of their clients. Listing agents have been sued in multiple-offer situations when they also had a buyer who eventually bought the property. You can imagine that the other agents were thinking things like, "Did you even present my offer?" or "Did you present my offer fairly?"

Presenting your offer in person as opposed to faxing it to the listing agent is also another visible way to demonstrate your value to your buyers. Presenting in person also shows your value to the seller. There can be unexpected benefits as well. For instance, one seller appreciated my professionalism in presenting an offer so much that, even though she didn't accept it, after her listing expired she asked me to sell her property, which I did. You just never know when your value will shine through.

100) BE ON TIME FOR APPOINTMENTS

When you are late for an appointment, it communicates to clients that you don't respect their time, which is another way of saying you don't value them. Respect is a two-way street. If you, as the professional, want to be treated with respect, you have to return the favor. How often do other professionals have a different rule for themselves than they do for the people who make an appointment with them? Think about how many times you sat in a doctor's or dentist's office waiting an hour or more, and you know perfectly well that if you were the one who was late, your appointment would have been cancelled. As real estate professionals, we cannot stay in business long without the goodwill of our clients, so we owe it to them to show that we hold their time to be just as valuable as our own.

Yet, for reasons that have never been clear to me, real estate agents seem to have a reputation for being unreliable. Being punctual is one of the fastest and easiest ways to establish your professionalism in the eyes of potential clients. And it's not hard to manage if you plan to arrive early, rather than trying to arrive exactly at the moment when you're due. An extra 15 minutes leaves plenty of room for traffic jams, getting lost, and last-minute interruptions and phone calls that habitually cause people to be late. I believe many people cut it close because they don't want to be without something to do should they arrive early. However, if you arrive early you can relax and either prepare for the client, or catch up on that book you've been meaning to read.

When I arrive early, I wait until about 10 minutes before the appointment and then knock on the client's door. When he opens it, I will actually apologize for being a bit early, which causes him to remember that not only was I on time, I was actually early. I believe this establishes straight off that clients have one reason, already, to believe I am reliable. Once they know they can rely on me, I have already started selling my value.

However, to establish real credibility, you must be punctual not just for your first appointment but for all the others after that. The nice thing is that if you are consistently on time, being late once in a while due to unforeseen circumstances will cause your clients to be much more forgiving than if you are always late.

Another benefit of being on time is that it reduces stress. When someone is late, her stress level rises with the slightest obstacle. She suddenly seems to catch every red light, to hit the heaviest traffic, and to find herself at an address that has no street parking whatsoever. These are occurrences that can happen to anyone, but they take on added tension when there isn't a second to spare. On the other hand, when you leave with plenty of time to get there, you don't even notice these little inconveniences because you have nothing to lose by hitting another red light.

101) HIRE AN ASSISTANT

Remember that the job of a real estate professional is to spend as much time as possible getting face-to-face with potential and current clients. Anything that takes away from that time should be done by someone else, if possible. The more face time you have with clients, the more value they perceive you to have, because they really don't appreciate the importance of paperwork.

There are two types of assistants: unlicensed and licensed. Unlicensed assistants are basically limited to clerical or secretarial duties such as the following*:

- Maintaining files
- Making appointments
- Mailing marketing materials
- Designing flyers
- Keeping client information current
- Helping to track business expenses
- Tracking incoming and outgoing referrals
- Inputting new client leads into database
- Making duplicate keys to a property
- Tracking progress in meeting goals in business plan
- Ordering "For Sale" signs for new listings
- Implementing FSBO follow-up programs
- Coordinating home staging services
- Placing advertising in various media
- Following up with the agent representing the buyer or seller on a transaction
- Hundreds of other duties limited only by your imagination

Because they are licensed as agents, licensed assistants can do, almost everything the agent can do such as the following:

- Prospecting
- Interviewing buyers

- Showing property to buyers
- Explaining contracts to buyers
- Explaining contracts to sellers
- Discussing the attributes of a property with a client
- Communicating with FSBOs and expired listings
- Hundreds of other duties limited only by your imagination

Much of the back office work in real estate could be done by an unlicensed assistant. Real estate is one of the most highly regulated industries in America and, as a result, there is an inordinate amount of paperwork required to comply with regulations and laws.

Remember that your assistant's time is tax deductible while yours is not. Any time someone can do a job as well or better than you for less money it makes financial sense. For example, if you earn $50 an hour and an assistant costs $15 an hour, after taxes you are netting $35 an hour.

How you compensate your assistant is up to you, depending on how much you want to motivate them. Here are some assistant compensation statistics from a 2005 survey by the National Association of REALTORS®:

- 37 percent are paid hourly
- 24 percent are paid a salary
- 15 percent receive a percentage of the commission
- 7 percent are paid by the task
- 17 percent have other arrangements

---

* Be sure to check your state and local real estate laws for any limitations.

Part Five

INCREASE YOUR VALUE WITH EDUCATION AND PROFESSIONAL DEVELOPMENT

102) TAKE A NEGOTIATING CLASS

Studies show that one of the few real estate services that our clients do appreciate and are willing to pay for is negotiating. Sellers know that a strong negotiator makes them money by getting them the highest price with the least amount of work on the house, minimizing their liability for any work that does need to be done, and convincing the buyers to pay for cosmetic repairs. Buyers are quite aware that a savvy haggler can save them big bucks by negotiating down the price on the home of their dreams, getting them the best terms and conditions, making sure the repairs are paid for by the seller, and possibly getting the seller to carry back a second loan.

People in America generally do not like to bargain because they're not used to it and it somehow seems pushy and rude. In other places like China, Mexico, and the Middle East, people negotiate on everything all day long, so they tend to be more experienced than we are. Americans might not want to negotiate themselves, but they certainly want the benefits that it can bring. They more than appreciate it if their real estate agent can speak forcefully on their behalf and hold their own at the bargaining table.

So if you want to get paid what you're worth, you must learn to become a superb negotiator. Taking a class will increase your skill and confidence at haggling for items both large and small on behalf of your clients.

In my book, *Black Belt Negotiating*, I show how some very simple principles that have been used for thousands of years can give you an edge when bargaining. In it, I lay out the seven steps to successful negotiating:

- **Step one:** Learn the basics. There are basic rules of bargaining, which must be mastered if you want to hold your own. It starts with not being afraid to bargain. Many of us are reluctant to even try because we're afraid to lose. But there is nothing to lose. There was no deal before you started and perhaps you will walk away empty-handed, so you really will have lost nothing. And who knows, you might surprise yourself and win.
- **Step two:** Conduct prefight preparation. You must learn everything about your opponent, the environment in which the negotiation will take place, and the property itself before you sit down at the bargaining table.
- **Step three:** Warmup. You must make the other party feel comfortable before starting the negotiations; that is likely to inspire a more positive attitude toward you.
- **Step four:** Round one of the negotiations. This is where the sparring begins with both sides making offers and counteroffers to see if their basic needs can be met. If not, they will walk away.
- **Step five:** Find middle ground. Here you make sure all your needs have been met and you start adding your wants.
- **Step six:** The close. You close the deal and congratulate the other party for having gotten such a good deal. Being gracious at this stage is crucial for cementing the deal; otherwise

the other party may back out later if he harbors regret or resentment.

- **Step seven:** Continuous improvement. After every bargaining session, top negotiators always take time to evaluate their performance and strive to become better.

What top negotiators learn is that bargaining doesn't just involve haggling over price. If you want to be successful, you must do your homework before the bargaining begins. This helps you develop a clear list of wants and needs, strategize a plan for presenting your client's situation in a sympathetic way (without revealing too much), develop effective counteroffers, and come up with creative solutions—skills which can all be learned.

Practice what you have learned in low risk venues such as garage sales and flea markets before you take it to the big tent—negotiating for a half-million dollar house. Practicing your newly developed skills as often as possible will make you a master and give you a considerable edge over the competition. Your clients will be thrilled when they see that they have a black belt in their corner, whereas the other side only has a street fighter.

In foreign countries, whenever you have a chance, watch how people there bargain. Observe their interactions carefully, especially in developing countries where money is precious. They don't bargain for the thrill of it, they bargain to put food on the table. You can imagine how motivated they are.

One of the first ways a seller will test the negotiating skill of a potential listing agent is to see if she will lower her commission. Many believe that if you cannot justify the value of your own services, you will not be able to bargain effectively on behalf of your client. And perhaps they have a point. Sell your value and don't lower your commission. Remember, people don't get what they deserve, they get what they negotiate.

103) TAKE A TAX CLASS

Knowing how taxes affect real estate transactions can really benefit your clients because they usually don't know much about taxes themselves. They will come to see you as a valuable resource in this important area. Buying and selling property in the United States can affect your clients' tax planning, as well as other aspects of their financial, investment, and estate situations.

Currently, tax laws enable single property owners to realize $250,000 in profit from the sale of their principal residence and pay no income tax. The amount is $500,000 for married couples who file jointly. Knowing the rules to qualify for this exclusion can have a major impact on the financial wealth of your clients.

A basic tax course will help you understand the tax benefits of home ownership, how holding title can affect taxation, the potential savings of capital gains treatment when you sell, as well as the nuances of taxes as they impact investment property.

One of the biggest benefits I got out of taking a tax class was learning about *tax-deferred exchanges.* Under Internal Revenue Service Code Section 1031, property that is held for investment—such as apartments, commercial buildings, strip shopping centers, and even raw land—can be exchanged with no current tax due. This enables your clients to take their profit out of one property and put it into investment property without having its buying power reduced by taxes at the time of sale. If they are not paying tax, they'll have more money to invest in the transaction.

A bonus is the fact that most investment property owners are not going to merely exchange one property for another of exactly the same price. They're familiar with the benefits of leverage, so they'll usually buy a property that is substantially higher in price than the one they are selling. This means that you do not just get the commissions on two transactions; you could earn several times that.

Taking a tax class doesn't necessarily mean you will be preparing income tax returns for clients, but it will give you more tools to help them gain the biggest benefit from their largest investment. Remember that when you buy and sell property for someone, whether as an investment or for personal use, it can affect their tax situation. Obviously, they should contact their own tax advisor before engaging in any complex real estate transaction.

104) EARN A REAL ESTATE DESIGNATION

A real estate designation tells clients that you are professional, believe in education, and are a cut above other agents. A designation can provide you with specialized knowledge and skills that can greatly benefit your clients.

According to the most recent National Association of REALTORS® study, less than 20 percent of all REALTORS® have earned the Graduate REALTOR® Institute (GRI) designation. This same study indicated that REALTORS® with this designation earned over $33,200 more annually than nondesignees. The GRI designation indicates to your clients that you have taken the time to obtain a higher level of education than most agents do.

Earning this designation is a benefit to you, too. The network of people you meet will help you generate more leads and referrals. The REALTOR® Institute is more than 25 years old and thousands have graduated from it. Those who do, find it to be a powerful tool for attracting and building new business. In today's competitive business environment, you need more than just motivation and initiative to succeed, you need the advantage of the education you receive in the GRI program and others. Don't forget to display your GRI designation proudly as a way to differentiate yourself from average agents.

Once you have earned this, consider moving on to get your Certified Residential Specialist (CRS) designation. There are only about 45,000 REALTORS® in business today who hold the CRS, which is about nine percent of all agents. This is not surprising since it is the highest designation in residential real estate.

CRS training gives agents in-depth knowledge about business planning, making listing presentations, negotiating and closing with smoother transactions, working in the buyers' and sellers' best interests, and building a referral business. Another huge benefit is the well-organized network, where one can refer and receive referrals from CRS designees all over the country. In fact, the usefulness of obtaining any professional designation is that it gives you the opportunity to network with other educationally minded agents.

Some of the other benefits of getting your CRS designation include access to local CRS chapters, a national convention known as "Sell-a-bration," and a monthly magazine. Studies show that the CRS designation is well worth the effort of attaining since graduates earn on average $50,000 more in commissions per year than other agents. Obtaining other designations—such as Certified Real Estate Brokerage Manager® (CRB), Certified Property Manager® (CPM), Accredited Buyer Representative (ABR), Seniors Real Estate Specialist® (SRES)—indicates that you believe in continuing education as a way to serve your clients better every year you're in business. It also separates you from your competitors who don't invest the time and money in attending classes. Just like the Certified Public Accountants (CPA) and Certified Financial Planners®(CFP) designations, real estate designations illustrate your professionalism and differentiate you from average agents.

Remember that in addition to the knowledge you'll gain, earning designations gives you the opportunity to network with other educationally minded agents. There are many opportunities to give and receive referrals withing these networks.

105) LEARN FINANCING OPTIONS TO HELP YOUR CLIENTS

Most agents leave the financing of real estate to the lender or mortgage broker. However, the more you know about financing, the more you can help your clients buy homes and investment properties.

Can you define the following financing terms?

- Reverse annuity mortgage
- Negative amortization loan
- Interest-only loan
- Seller buy-down
- Seller carryback
- FHA loan
- VA loan

Do you know the difference between the following financing providers?

- **Mortgage banker:** any lender with sufficient assets to originate loans and create pools of loans
- **Mortgage broker:** a broker of loans to wholesale lending institutions
- **Wholesale lender:** any person or entity who makes a mortgage loan or purchases or services mortgage loans
- **Portfolio lender:** an institution that lends its own money and originates loans for itself
- **Direct lender:** any institution that can fund its own loans
- **Correspondent:** a company that originates and closes home loans in its own name and usually then sells them to a larger lender, called a sponsor

- **Bank:** community, regional, or national for-profit business corporation owned by private investors and governed by a board of directors chosen by the stockholders
- **Savings and loan:** Usually a company that specializes in real estate financing. It can be either a corporation or mutual (a type of business where making a deposit is like purchasing stock in the organization). Both types are governed by an elected board of directors.
- **Credit union:** A nonprofit financial cooperative owned by its members and governed by a board of directors elected by, and from among, those members. Usually there is a common bond among the members, such as belonging to the same organization or living in the same geographical area. Credit unions accept deposits from their members and use them to make relatively short-term loans.

You should be at least familiar with the various financing options, including such terms as *reverse annuity mortgages, negative amortization loans, interest-only loans,* etc. There has been a lot of negative press about these terms in recent years and you should be aware of the pros and cons of the major financing options.

Remember, the key to home ownership for most people is financing, so you should have at least a basic working knowledge of the different loan programs available in your area. You can sit down with a knowledgeable loan broker who can help you.

There are hundreds of financing options, only a few of which will meet the needs of your client. There are many myths about financing, such as the fact that negative amortization or interest-only loans are bad. There are no bad loans as long as the client is appropriate.

Some of the most commonly used loans today include the following:

- Fixed rate
- Variable rate

- Negative amortization
- Fixed rate with conversion option to variable
- Variable rate with conversion option to fixed
- Owner financing
- FHA
- VA

Learn as much as you can about financing because it is the key to home ownership for most buyers. The more you know the more, you will be able to help them.

106) LIVE A BALANCED LIFE

To be of maximum service to your clients, you need to be alert, imaginative, and resourceful. You can't be at your best if your life is out of balance.

Making time for youself is not just a nice thing to do, it's essential to your success because it gives you time to rejuvenate from a very difficult business. It improves your mood and state of mind so you're more pleasant to work with. You need downtime to lower your stress levels so you can develop solutions to your professional challenges. Your clarity, focus, creativity, and problem-solving abilities will improve when all the other parts of your life are balanced and aligned. When you do return to working with clients, you will bring renewed energy and a more creative approach.

Success in real estate and in life is not about making a lot of money. I have had the privilege of addressing some of the top real estate agents in the world who make $2 million to $20 million a year and more. What I've noticed is that they generally take much more time off than the average agent because it helps them to be more relaxed and innovative, qualities they put to good use for their clients.

So living a balanced life is crucial to your well-being and your business. Remember that life is to live—not to work. No one ever said on their deathbed, "I wish I had spent more time showing property and on listing appointments."

You don't have to wait for a vacation to treat yourself. On a daily basis, find little ways to reward yourself for having done a good job. You might enjoy a long, hot bath or a scoop of your favorite ice cream. Plan time for having fun with your family, practicing your faith, keeping up your health, and continuing your education. On your calendar, write down the activities that support your priorities and keep the appointment to do them, just as you would an appointment with an important client—they are equally important.

Take at least one day off a week. You need the rest and your clients will get along without you. If you have to be at open houses on Sunday, then take off Monday. Just touch base with clients before your day off so there's no need for them to phone you on your special day.

In addition, take at least two weeks off every year. I have found that I am never more creative about my business and I'm never able to solve more problems than when I'm sitting on the deck of a cruise ship! The real estate profession is more time intensive and emotionally draining than most careers, so two weeks is probably not sufficient for most agents.

And don't forget to celebrate the joyous events in your life, like birthdays, anniversaries, and graduations. And celebrate work milestones, too. I don't just mean closed transactions, but major milestones such as getting a farm established, publishing your first newsletter, or kicking off a new marketing campaign.

Think of the parts of your life as the spokes of a wheel. When your life is in balance, the spokes are the same length, but when some aspects are overemphasized and others are neglected, you get a wheel that is lopsided and doesn't roll smoothly. Just as a wheel cannot roll unless it is balanced, neither can your life. Once you see where you could use balance, design a plan to add more of what you need in your life. Use the ideas in this book to provide accountability for accomplishing balance.

It may seem like a contradiction, that success in real estate and in life is not about making a lot of money, but I have found that the most financially successful people in our profession also seem to have the most balance in their lives. Is this a coincidence? I think not.

107) HIRE A COACH

If you are constantly worried about building your practice, looking for business, and holding deals together, you cannot provide the best service to current clients. Coaching can increase your confidence, increase your business success, and allow you to concentrate on providing stellar service.

More top agents than ever are hiring coaches to help them with their personal and professional lives. First, a coach will help you balance your life, which ultimately benefits your clients. Second, a coach makes your business run better, which means you have more time and energy to serve clients' unique needs.

The job of a coach is to help you develop, clarify, and reach your goals. Coaching has become very popular because it's all about you. Your coach's guidance is focused completely on your needs to help you develop, clarify, and reach your goals. If you are doing all this, what does the coach do?

Just as in sports, coaches stand on the sidelines and provide guidance and direction. For example, a coach might ask you, "What's the one goal you would like to achieve that would really help your career?" If you say that you'd like to develop a physical farm, the coach might ask, "What would be the first step in setting up a farm?" You would have to think about it, and then perhaps you would respond that you have an area in mind, but you need more information. Coach: "Where could you get this information?" You: "The title company." I think you can guess the next question. Coach: "Which title company?" You: "I do a lot of business with ABC Title, so I could call them." Coach: "So is contacting ABC Title something you'd be willing to do to get your farm started?" If you say yes, then the coach would likely say, "By when do you think you could contact them?" You might counter with a date that's two weeks later, to which the coach would say, "So, is it okay if I ask you about it in two weeks to see how it's going?" If you say yes, the coach will note it in her calendar and ask you about it in two weeks.

You can see from this example that setting up a farm was your idea and all the coach did was guide you toward taking the first step. Once you finished the clarification process, the coach helped you develop an action plan and form a deadline. In the end, she provided accountability because that's where the real power of coaching lies. The same principle is why Weight Watchers works. When you know someone is going to ask whether you have dropped two pounds, as you said you would, you are far more likely to avoid that box of popcorn at the movies. Without the oversight, we drop our action steps left and right.

The goal is yours all along and even the way to accomplish it is of your choosing. Coaching works because you are heading toward goals that you set up in a way that is most appropriate to you. No one forces anything on you. If you don't achieve what you intended, it's no one's fault but your own.

You can certainly find coaches on the Internet, but the best way to locate one who is competent is to ask for a referral from another agent. A coach does not necessarily need to know anything about the real estate profession to be of service. However, if you are looking for mentoring and coaching, find someone who is knowledgeable about our profession. The difference between a coach and a mentor is that a mentor tells you how to reach your goals. He may use his experience to provide options for you to choose from. If you work with a masterful mentor, it will work wonders for your relationship with your clients because you'll be of more and more use to them whenever they ask for help.

108) FORM A MASTERMIND GROUP

Forming a mastermind group is like giving your clients their very own think tank. One way of looking at this is that your client then has a brain trust, not just one person working for her on a transaction. You will be able to brainstorm solutions to difficult problems with the members of your group, and they'll provide essential experience for you to draw from when you have questions outside your area of expertise. These people help generate ideas for selling problem properties and dealing with contract issues, for example. Real estate can be a lonely profession, and the complexities of it are sometimes overwhelming. A mastermind group can give you support, encouragement, and additional resources.

They say that two heads are better than one. If so, then six minds are certainly better than two. Regularly convene a group of like-minded, noncompeting agents in your area to exchange ideas, share success stories, and talk about issues of mutual interest. Forming a mastermind group is one of the fastest ways to catapult your career to the next level because you are giving yourself a brand new source of creative ideas for improving your business.

A group like this gives you the opportunity to brainstorm with your peers about anything that is holding you back. It provides ideas about ways to accomplish a new goal, such as souping up a marketing campaign or extending your target area.

Just a few of the topics of discussion could include the following:

- Dealing with difficult clients
- Developing a farm
- Learning about new tax laws affecting real estate
- Investigating interest rate changes
- Adapting to changing market conditions

You can bounce new ideas off of your group before you implement them, or have the group help you figure out how to close with a particularly stubborn seller. As a bonus, they can be an additional source of referrals.

Another benefit of having a mastermind group is increased accountability. You share your goals with each other and ask people in the group to make sure you take the necessary steps to achieve those goals.

The following are the rules for forming a mastermind group:

- The group must be relatively small. Generally five to six is about the maximum number of people who can reasonably share issues in a couple of hours.
- Members must be at a similar level in their careers. If some are too advanced, they usually end up mentoring the others and get very little out of it themselves. If some are too new in the business, they will slow the process with very elementary questions and issues.
- Members must have similar goals for joining the group.
- You must meet on a regular basis (monthly, every other month, once a quarter).
- Attendance is mandatory. Set a limit on the maximum number of meetings a member of the group can miss annually.
- Everyone must share and participate.
- Confidentiality must be maintained at all times.

Any time competitors get together, there is the possibility of violating antitrust laws. These were established to ensure fair competition and avoid collusion in the marketplace. A group of real estate professionals in a room sharing war stories and business ideas could be misconstrued by a suspicious mind. The best way to avoid any appearance of impropriety is to keep in mind that while members of a mastermind group can share ideas and issues, they cannot encourage anyone to do as they do, like charge the same rate of commission or avoid doing business with a competitor.

109) LEARN TO MASTER TIME

The agent who is always running late, doesn't return phone calls, has to do paperwork in a hurry (paperwork is a huge part of real estate), rushes clients through the home search process, hastily answers questions, or races through the client's concerns and worries will not win many points with clients. The client is ill served and likely feels his agent always has something better to do.

Success in real estate requires that you use time efficiently and effectively so you always have the time to serve the client well. We don't sell real estate, but rather we sell our time; properties are only a vehicle. Being efficient with our time means squeezing every minute out of every day, which is difficult because there is a tremendous amount of wasted time in this field. We all waste it by doing the following:

- Waiting for clients
- Driving to and from client meetings
- Driving to and from the office
- Sitting in open houses waiting for potential buyers
- Working with unmotivated sellers
- Working with unmotivated buyers
- Talking unnecessarily on the phone
- Responding to unimportant email

Some time wasters are out of our control. Others, however, can be eliminated if we identify the culprit and then work around it. If you cannot eliminate a certain task, find a way to be productive anyway by multitasking. For instance, you might read a real estate magazine or the real estate section of the newspaper while holding a house open, or you could listen to educational CDs while driving.

Some time wasters can be controlled. One of the easiest is not to take listings or clients outside your geographical service area. Another technique is to group all your calls and emails together. Studies show that doing these kinds of activities all at one time greatly increases efficiency because you are mentally focused on a single task; you don't need to keep picking up and putting down the phone or mouse. And you don't need to switch your mindset to a new activity, which takes up more time and causes stress. Studies show that people who have to switch attention all day are more tired after eight hours.

The key to real time mastery is to plan your day the night before, by making a list of activities you want to accomplish and then deciding on the most efficient order in which to accomplish them. Planning in advance enables you to group activities together in a way that makes sense. While you're already in your office, make sure you do everything that can only be done there. When you're passing through downtown, have a list of stops you have to make in that area. When you have to visit a client at her house, make sure you bring everything with you that you'll need.

Another secret to controlling your time is to always give yourself a deadline; it doesn't matter what you are doing. As mentioned earlier, a deadline is usually the soonest you will ever complete a task. So setting limits means you will finish that task in a more timely way. If you're writing a letter to a client and you think it will take 30 minutes, give yourself only 20 minutes and see how far you get. You'll be surprised how much you can accomplish when you push yourself by setting aggressive deadlines.

There are certain time-saving techniques that can be particularly useful to real estate professionals. Here are just a few of them:

- Use form letters. Much of what we do in real estate is very repetitive, so keep copies of commonly used letters in your computer and just change the date and specifics. Why reinvent the wheel for each new client?
- Do the most difficult work when you're at your best. Some of us are more effective in the morning, others are better at midday, and still others are at the top of our game at night. If you are a night owl, write contracts in the evening. Do research when you are most alert at night.

- Hire an assistant to do paperwork and other repetitive tasks. A successful real estate professional should spend most of his or her time meeting with clients. Remember also that an assistant's time is tax deductible whereas yours is not.
- Have breakfast or lunch with clients. You have to meet with clients and you need to eat, so why not combine the two activities? In addition, meetings over meals can be tax deductible. (See your tax advisor for details.)
- Take a time management class. If you don't have time for one, you *really* need one!

110) IF YOU BELIEVE IN REAL ESTATE—BUY IT

How would you feel about a Mercedes salesperson who drove a Lexus? You'd wonder how much faith she had in her product, wouldn't you? It's the same in real estate.

Obviously, the first piece of property you should buy is your own home. How would clients look at you if you rented an apartment? If you don't yet own a home, set your sights on an area where you would like to live and decide what style of house you would prefer. Then, talk to a lender about how much down payment and earnings you would need to qualify for properties in this price range. Once you have achieved these two goals, just wait for the right house to hit the market and buy it. You can see the added advantage—this experience will help you better empathize with your buyers.

Once you've purchased your own home, the next goal should be to buy an investment property. Few investments have the potential for such large returns—as well as tax benefits—as real estate. Where else can you invest only 20 or 30 percent of the value, and receive tax deductions and potential appreciation from 100 percent of the investment? That's the beauty of investing in real estate! In addition, when you sell, you should be entitled to special capital gains tax rates, which can save you even more money.

The experience you will gain from buying and selling your own investment properties will teach you how to help clients defer taxes on investments using Internal Revenue Service Code Section 1031 exchanges. Many of your commercial property owners would be very interested in this technique. Personally, I found my investment properties to be the best retirement vehicle. I would hate to think where I'd be after 30 years of real estate if I had not consistently invested in real estate over all of that time.

One benefit of being in the real estate profession is that, because we are constantly working in the market, we are often exposed to deals on property that our clients may not want, but ones that would make solid investments for ourselves. Contact a tax specialist who is familiar with real estate and the tax impacts of investments on real estate professionals. There are special rules for people in our profession.

111) BUILD A BUSINESS, NOT JUST TRANSACTIONS

Successful agents take a long-term view and build a complete business so clients can count on them for years to come. Less successful agents take the shortsighted approach of just flitting from one transaction to another without any sense of direction. The former provides a reliable and predictable income flow, while the latter is very mercurial and shifty. In other words, treat your business as a business, not a hobby. It's not something you can just play at part-time.

So how do you build a business? The first step is to develop a business plan that gives you clear and measurable targets for the number and type of transactions you need in order to reach your goals. This lets you forecast what your income and expenses will be for the year as well as track them to see how you're doing at any given point. At the end of every year, sit down with your broker and your family to figure out your income and personal goals for the coming year.

The following are the major components of a standard business plan:

- Objectives
- Mission
- Services you will offer
- Market analysis
- Market segmentation
- Target market segmentation strategy
- Marketing plan
- Strategy and implementation
- Unique selling proposition
- Sales forecast
- Checkpoints
- Financial plan
- Break-even analysis
- Projected profit and loss

Your business plan should be evaluated on a regular basis; for many, it's every three months. It helps establish if you are on target to reach your goals. If not, what action will you take to get back on track?

Next, develop a marketing plan that brings you plenty of clients. Use different media outlets to target your most likely clients in venues that are most likely to reach them. This gives you the opportunity to work with people who are serious and reject the ones who will waste your time. As with the business plan, the marketing plan should be regularly evaluated against specific and measurable targets. You also want to examine the impact of any new marketing campaigns and advertising media so you can stick with what works and disregard the rest.

Your business plan should also include a regular schedule of educational programs to improve your skills and knowledge. This is a complex and constantly changing business. It takes a certain amount of work just to maintain yourself at your level. If you want to actually build your business and prosper, you need to do even more. Continuing education is your way of staying ahead of the curve, spotting trends, and finding newer services to provide to your clients.

A smart businessperson does not rely on just one source of income. Many large companies in the 1970s went bankrupt when they lost their sole source of income—government contracts. As a real estate professional, you are in a business that is notorious for its starts and stops in income. So you want to develop multiple streams of income, which will help smooth out the peaks and valleys of revenue flow. For instance, consider offering property management services for clients who own income property. Not only can this give you a regular monthly income, but when it comes time for the owner to sell, you are in the best position to be the listing agent. You're the one who knows the property, the tenants, and the owner better than anyone else.

Other sources of income could include the following:

- Real estate consulting
- Real estate expert witness work
- Real estate radio talk show host
- Real estate television talk show host
- Selling subscriptions to your real estate newsletter

GIVE THEM MORE THAN THEY EXPECT

You can really build value fast by giving your clients more than they expect. In keeping with that practice, I am giving you more than 111 ways to justify your commission.

112) EMPATHIZE WITH YOUR CLIENTS

We sell and buy real estate for clients nearly every day and for us it's nothing terribly challenging or exciting. We often forget that for clients, just walking into our offices can be a traumatic experience. They have no idea who we are or if we are reputable.

If it's the first time a buyer has ever bought a home, she is afraid to make a mistake with such a large purchase. If it's the first time an owner has ever sold a home, he is afraid of paying too much in commission for the services he is going to receive.

Demonstrating empathy puts the person at ease by letting her know that you hear and understand her fears, and that you're there to help in any way you can. It especially inspires faith if you tell the client how you dealt with such problems in the past.

For instance:

Buyer: "I'm very nervous that the monthly payments will be too high for me."

Agent: "Yes, these can be a bit frightening at first. When I bought my first house, the payments scared me to death. However, after I made up a budget I could see that, while things would be tight for a while, I could manage to make the payments without too much trouble. Why don't we do a quick budget and see how we can make this easy for you?"

Focus on the clients and listen from their perspective. In other words, put yourself in their shoes.

113) BEAT STRESS BEFORE IT BEATS YOU

As I've said many times in this book, real estate is a stressful profession—for the agent and the client. The last thing a client wants is for you to add your stress to his. He has enough on his plate. It is your responsibility to handle your own tensions before they ever reach the client. Don't wait until you are edgy, short-tempered, and harried to take a break.

According to a television news survey, sales is one of the most stressful occupations, just behind information technology, medical care, and engineering. I would submit that of all the sales jobs, selling real estate is one of the most stressful because it is such a large transaction.

Now a little stress can actually be positive in that it can make our lives more interesting and fun. It takes the edge off boredom. This is why roller coasters are so popular across the country. If you didn't think there was a possibility you could die, you wouldn't experience the thrill of absolute fear, which produces the adrenaline rush people are paying for. But too much stress for prolonged periods hurts you both psychologically and physically. It can also lower your self-esteem, reduce your effectiveness, raise your blood pressure, cause heart attacks, and even result in death. In Japan, there are so many deaths every year from the stress of overwork that they actually have a word for it—*karoshi*.

Stress can build slowly so that you hardly notice it until it's too late. So you have to constantly be alert to the following danger signs:

- Feeling anxious or irritable
- Mood swings
- Low self-esteem
- Fear of failure
- Difficulty concentrating
- Forgetfulness
- Grinding your teeth
- Loss of appetite
- Overeating

Life events that automatically raise your stress levels above what our profession normally imposes include the following:

- The death of a loved one
- Relocation
- Divorce
- Lawsuits
- Marriage
- Moving into a leadership position
- Major injury or illness in your life or those close to you
- Financial problems
- Moving residences

So, how do you beat stress? First, learn to say no. Say no to clients who ask for too much, especially on your off-hours, especially if they don't appreciate you. I know we all like to be nice and pitch in whenever possible, but you have to set boundaries and when they are violated, turn down the request. Then clients know when they can call you without worrying about it. By managing their expectations, you take the anxiety out of the process.

We are all different. We react to different stressors in our own way, so we have to cure ourselves in our own way. You can read books and listen to authorities, but you're the one who best knows how to relax yourself. Many agents relax with meditation and breathing exercises, while others find a round of golf rejuvenating. However you choose to do it, take a break from stress. If you are at work and involved in a situation you can't just abandon, like in a long negotiation, take yourself out of it even if it's only for a few minutes. The easiest tactic is to say you need a bathroom break. But try to build in natural breaks throughout the day. Do what the Europeans do and turn lunch into an event. They don't just grab a hot dog, they sit down with a glass of wine and a good meal and enjoy themselves for about two hours. In fact, they think the American idea of eating a sandwich at their desks is crazy. Everyone needs time throughout their busy, chaotic days to give their nerves a rest.

You can also reduce stress by setting realistic goals for yourself. Posing an unrealistic goal is like having a demanding parent standing over you and expecting you to perform far beyond your capacity. If it is impossible to whittle a mountain of paperwork down in an hour, you are just setting yourself up for disappointment. While goal-setting is crucial to your success, be sure you're aiming for something that's within reason given your past history, your innate capacity, and the current state of your market. You can't sell a broken-down house in a scary neighborhood in a buyers' market, when fantastic houses in safe neighborhoods aren't even selling. Your only goal in a situation like this should be to do your best. You can always do that much.

You've heard this before, but it always bears repeating: Delegate as much as you can to others. You don't have to be this overworked. An assistant (see Tip #101) or office mate can handle much of the work that could be causing you stress. Don't get overwhelmed by all the details required by our profession—delegate them.

Take all the vacation time you can. If the average worker in the United States gets 13 days of vacation, shouldn't someone in a high-stress job like real estate take much more time off? Put vacations and other rest days into your calendar and keep these appointments just as diligently as you would a meeting with an important client—in this case, that client is you.

114) UNDERSTAND THE DECISION-MAKING PROCESS

Our clients must justify their decisions to buy or sell, not only to themselves, but to others who will be affected, such as friends and family. We can show them how to sell the benefits of their actions if we understand how decisions are made.

Decision making is how people choose a course of action from among a group of alternatives. Understanding this process can not only help you recognize opportunities but also make the job easier for your clients.

The first step in the process is to define the problem. What need is the person trying to fill by buying or selling a property? This is where strong questioning and listening skills play an important role because the answer sets up what you do next.

There are a number of clarifying questions you can ask to help make the issue clearer in the client's mind, such as the following:

- Why do you want to buy/sell?
- By when do you need to buy/sell?
- Who will be affected by this decision?
- How will they feel about it?

To move forward, the client must gather all the facts needed to make an informed choice. Obviously, real estate professionals can be extremely helpful in making sure that all the appropriate data is available, but they shouldn't provide so much information that it overwhelms the client. Ask yourself the following questions:

- What specific information is needed to make the decision?
- What data should I leave out?
- Where could I obtain the necessary information?
- How would I use it?

The next step is brainstorming possible options and solutions. You provide an objective opinion from your experience. Next, the client considers and compares the pros and cons of each option. This is where other professionals like accountants and attorneys might be consulted.

Finally, the client selects the best option for him. This is the closing process. Using effective closing techniques can be very helpful at this stage. Remember, given the choice to do what's in his best interests or do nothing, he will probably do nothing without help from you. You have to help him sift through everything he has reviewed and use it to make the choice you know he really wants to make, but is afraid to. Consider asking these questions:

- What will happen if you don't buy/sell?
- Will you be better off if you don't buy/sell?

Once the client does make a choice, he must explain his decision to those who are affected, like his children and friends. Sometimes this step is confusing or intimidating. Show him how to sell the benefit of his actions to others. He can start by asking himself what's in it for them. Once he has that figured out, he knows how to pitch his case so they see the advantages and support his choice.

115) PROVIDE EXCEPTIONAL CUSTOMER SERVICE

Everyone talks about customer service. Yet when was the last time you received really stellar service? Pretty rare, isn't it?

The beautiful thing about people having such a low opinion of real estate professionals is that it isn't hard to blow clients away with customer service that is only above average (since average is pretty low). Obviously, we should strive to do even better than above average, but you can see that this is a huge opportunity.

There are three possible responses whenever we interact with clients. The first is disappointment, which means we failed to meet their expectations. With the bar set so low for agents, if a client does feel this way, it is inexcusable. The next reaction is satisfaction, which means that you met their expectations but didn't go beyond them. This should be the bare minimum response we receive. When it's over and the client is only satisfied, it ought to provoke you to wonder what you could have done better. The third possible experience is delight, which means you far exceeded their expectations. The third response should be the goal of every agent.

If you follow the suggestions in this book, you are guaranteed to earn rave reviews from your clients and receive plenty of referrals. If you want to delight your clients, just remember to do the following:

- Return calls and emails promptly.
- Demonstrate your value at every opportunity.
- Educate your clients about the complexities of real estate transactions, so they see how much of a service you provide and realize they couldn't possibly do that for themselves.
- Under-promise and over-deliver.
- Stay in touch with them on a regular basis.
- Do the unexpected.
- Anticipate their needs and then meet them.

116) OFFER CLIENTS FREE MARKETING MATERIALS

How would you like free advertising all over your town at all times of the day and night? Just give your clients items they can use on a regular basis and they'll do the marketing for you. The key, of course, is that your name has to be all over them.

The most common thing salespeople give customers are pens with their names and phone numbers. The problem is that so many groups, including hotels, give free pens that they're no longer very effective as a marketing tool. As always, it pays to be unique.

Think about what you could give that clients would use all the time to advertise you. I don't give calendars because everyone else does, but I do give refrigerator magnets where clients can write their doctor's phone number and other important information. Obviously, it has my name and contact information on it as well.

The bags you give to buyers to put their Buyers' Kit in should have your name prominently featured, so while they are out looking at property they are simultaneously marketing you. I've even seen agents give their clients license plate holders. Now that's a satisfied client who would put one of these on her car!

Any specialty advertising supplier would be happy to send you a free catalog of items that can be given to clients. Think about what your clients would use on a regular basis and see if there is some kind of novelty that would fill that need.

Some of the more practical items I have found include the following:

- Travel mugs
- Magnifying glasses
- Organizers with pad, pen, and calculator
- Baseball caps and sun visors
- Umbrellas
- Frisbees for the kids
- Small flashlights

- Calculators

Some top agents across the country offer buyers and sellers a free moving van to use for local moves. It's not only a much appreciated service, but it acts as a powerful marketing tool because their name and contact information on both sides of the truck is being driven all over town.

117) KNOW YOUR COMPETITION

Any smart business owner knows his competition, and a real estate professional should be no different. What are the names of the handful of agents with whom you always find yourself in competition for listings? What are their strengths and weaknesses? What are their pricing structures? What are their personalities like? How do they brand themselves? Once you have ascertained all this, use it as a guideline to see how you can do better.

What do you do differently that serves your clients better than your competition? As much as you can, gather materials from your competitors. If you can't get on their mailing lists perhaps you have a friend, relative, or client who can pass their information along to you.

What kind of listing presentations do your competitors give? Do they use a laptop or flip book? What is their approach and style? Do they like to be the first agent to present or the last? Again, note their strengths and weaknesses.

How do your competitors work with buyers? Do they have clients sign a Buyer-Broker Agreement or not? Are they efficient at showing property?

When making offers on properties what are your competitors' styles? Are their contracts well written? Do they write them by hand or using software? Do they like to present offers in person or do they just drop them off or fax them in? What do they do in multiple-offer situations?

How do your competitors handle offers on their listings? Do they usually allow agents to present their offers in person? How do they handle multiple-offer situations?

The answers to all of these questions will give you ammunition for handling your competition. Where they are strong, you need to be just as strong. Where they are weak, you really need to shine.

There's nothing wrong with being cordial with your competitors. After all, that is the professional thing to do. In a sense, they really aren't your competitors, because somewhere down the road you will likely have a listing that they have a buyer for and vice versa. Without a little friendly competition none of us would survive for long.

118) BUILDING TRUST: A TWO-WAY STREET

During the course of a real estate transaction, you are going to be asking your clients for a great deal of personal and private information. When working with buyers, it isn't unusual to ask, "How much do you make?" or "Have you ever had a bankruptcy?" or "How much do you have saved up for a down payment?" When working with sellers it would be common to ask, "How much do you owe on this house?" or "Have you done any repairs without permits?" or "Are all of your loan payments and property tax bills current?" These are not casual questions you would ask a stranger at a cocktail party. They are, in fact, rather personal.

Before they share these and other intimate details of their lives they will need to trust you. The quickest way to inspire the trust it takes to give over personal information is for you to share a little information of your own. Go beyond your real estate resume, which states how long you've been in the business and how many transactions you've closed. You must be willing to share a bit of who you are—your background as well as your hopes and dreams. Trust begets trust. Besides, people want to do business with a human being they can relate to, not the model of the perfect real estate sales professional.

What you choose to share is up to you, but I start by telling my clients about my family, my hobbies of hiking and flying a small plane, and my passion for reading. Talk about whatever is comfortable and natural to you because the goal here is to build a rapport and make people comfortable with talking about themselves.

The biggest challenge with sharing part of your life is knowing where the boundary lies. If you share too much you will achieve the opposite of what you want—you will make people uncomfortable. And don't forget that this boundary changes depending upon where you live. In California, people think nothing of relating what they talked to their therapist about that afternoon. In South Carolina, they might not even tell you that they have a therapist.

In theory, there's a clear line between real estate and psychology, although in our profession that line often becomes blurred, especially in divorce cases and other stressful situations. Sometimes when people start talking about themselves to someone who is a very good listener, they cross the line without knowing it. Your role is to let them disclose whatever they're comfortable with disclosing. Listening with empathy to someone's problems builds trust like nothing else.

Just bear in mind that this is still a business relationship, albeit a close one. I have different levels of friends: a very few intimate friends with whom I can share my innermost thoughts, some close friends that I see on a regular basis, and then there are clients whom I see periodically in various settings. I am certainly closer to my clients than my masseuse or the guy who does my copying, because many of them have shared intimate details about their lives.

119) BECOME A CELEBRITY IN YOUR LOCAL AREA

Another way to quickly brand yourself is to become a celebrity in your local area. The way to do this is by being visible through such techniques as writing a column for your local newspaper, hosting a local radio or television real estate show, and gaining visibility being involved with a charity.

Our local board of REALTORS® has a monthly real estate television show and I host a segment called "Ask the Expert," where viewers can submit questions and I will answer them on the air. Friends and clients in our area constantly comment about the show and ask me questions about real estate because I am associated with the show.

One of my agent friends, MaryAnn DeGuzman, hosts her own local real estate radio program in the San Francisco Bay Area, where she interviews local agents about various aspects of buying and selling homes. Not only does she get lots of referrals from the guests on her show, but people consider her a real estate expert because of the program.

My articles have been featured in everything from our local hometown newspaper to the *Wall Street Journal.* They have have also been featured in our state association of REALTORS® magazine and on the cover of the National Association of REALTORS® magazine. I always get lots of comments from agents and clients about my writing and a lot more people know my name because of it.

To place an article in your local newspaper, contact the real estate editor with a brief note asking if he or she would be interested in your subject. Then include the article and a photo of yourself. The procedure is the same for magazines. Always save copies of your published articles in a publicity file. I like to copy them onto thick, glossy paper and give them out as promotional material.

To be a guest on a radio or television show, simply contact the host or producer of the program you want to appear on and let them know the topic you believe would be of interest to their listeners/viewers. Always ask for an air check of your show, which is nothing more than a copy of the show you were on. Get permission to use clips of the program for publicity purposes and to put them on your website. Nothing provides credibility faster than hearing or seeing a clip of someone on a radio or TV program.

120) LOVE WHAT YOU DO OR GET OUT!

Buying and selling a home can be a troublesome, frustrating, and stressful process, so working with an agent who projects confidence, goodwill, and a genuine love of his work is crucial to offset the negatives. He who exudes a calming and reassuring influence can make the whole transaction a lot less distressful. People love to work with people who love their jobs because the enthusiasm is contagious. I could never have stayed in the real estate profession for over three decades if I didn't love it and if I wasn't able to have fun with it.

As you can imagine, a crucial requirement for loving this business is working with people you like. Likeable clients make the work fun and enjoyable, whereas disagreeable types make it a tedious chore no matter how much they pay you. A day spent with an unpleasant person feels about 48 hours long.

Another way to increase the enjoyment of the business is to have a sense of humor. I know that for-sale-by-owners are usually going to be arrogant, so I have fun by sending them letters that tweak their noses a bit. For example, one of my letters is sent about six weeks into the marketing of their house, when most buyers have lost interest and not a lot is happening. The headline reads FEELING LONELY? Another example is the last letter I send two weeks later, which is hand-delivered and wrapped around a dry salami, and says, "No baloney! I can sell your house."

One key to loving your job that not many people think about is to focus on your clients, not the money. Doing any job strictly because it pays better than other work is the fastest road to burnout that I know. If your primary goal is to help your clients solve their problems, you will love this business until the day you retire.

Think about the significance of what we do. First, we put people in homes. If you ask most people in America who rent, they will tell you that more than anything, they aspire to own their own home someday. Why? Because it's a wonderful thing to come home from work and settle into a place that you can call your own; to plant a sapling in the front yard and know you'll still be there when it's a full-grown tree; or to paint the walls or add a bathroom and not have to ask the landlord for permission. When you raise children in your own home, it takes on a special significance. You can go into the kitchen and look at the notch in the doorframe that tells you how tall your college-age son was when he was five. A home has memories.

Another source of satisfaction is how we solve problems for our clients. This is one of the most important transactions of a person's life, and certainly it is his biggest investment. While it's obviously not brain surgery, it is a vital financial operation. Matching the right client, along with his family, to the right home is an awesome responsibility that I trust you recognize. Once people move in, it is unlikely they'll be able to move again for a long time, so it is truly important that they are comfortable with their choice. You play a big role in the choice they make.

Striking an overall balance is crucial; if you work too much or too hard, you'll find it difficult to love the job that is demanding too much of you. The real estate profession is not an end in itself but rather the means to an end. It sustains the lifestyle you have created and want to create in the future. Don't get so involved in the business that you neglect the rest of your life—family, physical exercise, mental growth, and spiritual exploration—all the aspects of life that make it worth living.

Learn to manage stress. Real estate is an extremely stressful profession and you will not love it for long if you are constantly in a state of tension because you can't stand your clients or coworkers, or you aren't making enough money, or you don't know what you're doing so you have to bluff, or you're overworked.

Continue to grow intellectually. Take classes and keep moving up, expanding your knowledge. Besides the obvious benefits to your clients, it will make the job more interesting to you. Even after all of these years in the business and learning about taxation as well as financial planning, I can see that I still have a lot to learn about our profession.

Have a positive attitude. Every real estate career has highs and lows. Things seem to move along smoothly and then we hit turbulence. Keep in mind the big picture that most transactions that are started eventually come to a successful closing. You don't need a positive attitude when you're up, you need it when you're down. It helps carry you over until the momentum picks up again.

If it's no longer fun . . . get out. There is no shame in leaving a job you don't enjoy anymore, no matter what it is. Doctors leave the medical profession every day just as attorneys leave the law. They may have spent years training, but it's no justification for staying longer than they want to. The biggest shame is feeling trapped in a job you hate to go to every day of your life. It's much like being in prison, except prisoners have to stay. You could leave any time you want but you don't. What a horrible thought!

So ask the ultimate question: "If I didn't get paid to do this job would I still do it?" If the answer is no, it's time to start planning an exit strategy.

Conclusion

So now that you've read this book, what are the next steps? Top agents don't just come up with great ideas after reading books or attending seminars. They consistently implement ideas by developing systems for putting them into action. Any idea is useless unless you make it happen in the real world. As mentioned previously, we are far more likely to act on a goal if we have to account for our accomplishment to another person.

Every New Year's, people make resolutions they don't keep because they are missing one important component—accountability. Top agents have others hold them accountable for accomplishing goals they want to reach. They will work harder to avoid looking like a slacker to a respected colleague, if for no other reason.

I'm sure you've read at least one idea in this book that could immediately increase your income. The first step to using it in your own business is to determine what is needed to make that idea a reality. For instance, let's say you like the idea of getting sponsors for your real estate newsletter so you can print and send it at no cost to you. The first thing you will need to do is find a way to have the newsletter written for you. You might contact companies who write such publications for REALTORS®. Next, you need to decide how many newsletters you want to send and how many pages it will be. This will determine the number of ads you need to cover the cost of writing, printing, and mailing, as well as selling ads. Then, you might want to hire someone to obtain the sponsors for your newsletter.

Since the first step to implementing the free newsletter idea is hiring a salesperson, you might decide a specific date by which you want him or her to start work. Then ask an office mate or a friend to remind you about it as the deadline approaches. If, for example, you want to have the salesperson start in a month, have someone in your mastermind group ask you how the hiring process is going in about two weeks. If no one has been hired by that time, that person should ask you for a status report in another week. This constant reminder makes you accountable for taking the steps necessary to accomplish your goal. In other words, you can't afford to drop the ball because others are watching.

With every activity in this book that you want to accomplish, follow this system:

1. Identify the goal.
2. Determine the steps needed to accomplish the goal.
3. Assign a deadline for the completion of the first step.
4. Assign a deadline for the completion of each subsequent step.
5. Ask someone to hold you accountable for meeting each deadline.

The goal of becoming a successful real estate professional is absolutely achievable if you break it down into one step at a time. This book has given you tips, ideas, and actions that you can use to make yourself into a top notch agent or broker and to get paid what you are worth. With a little effort, ambition, and creativity, what is there to stop you?

Michael Soon Lee, MBA, CRS, GRI, is one of the top real estate speakers and authors in the country, and he has been privileged to influence and inspire thousands. He has been licensed since 1977 and, as an agent, has earned as much as $75,000 in commissions *in one month*. As a broker, he has managed both large franchised firms with over 50 agents, as well as small independent companies.

Michael has spoken at nine National Association of REALTORS® conventions as well as for the Women's Council of REALTORS® convention, the Council of Residential Specialists convention, and at state association conventions including the following: California Association of REALTORS®, New Jersey Association of REALTORS®, Colorado Association of REALTORS®, Texas Association of REALTORS®, Missouri Association of REALTORS®, Wisconsin REALTORS® Association, and many others. He has also presented programs for companies such as Coldwell Banker, Prudential Real Estate, Jenny Pruitt and Associates, CTX Mortgage, Pardee Homes, Engle Homes, Coca-Cola, General Motors, and hundreds of others.

Michael is also the author of numerous books, audio CDs, and manuals, including *OPENING DOORS: Selling to Multicultural Real Estate Clients* and *Black Belt Negotiating*. He was president of the North San Mateo County Association of REALTORS®, a director for the California Association of REALTORS®, a director for the National Association of REALTORS®, and served for three years on the Educational Services Advisory Committee of the California Association of REALTORS®. He can be reached at (800) 417-7325, and his website is: www.SeminarsUnlimited.com.

Babitsky, Steven. *How to Become a Dangerous Expert Witness: Advanced Techniques and Strategies.* Falmouth, MA: SEAK, Inc., 2005.

Council of Residential Specialists. "Designation." http://www.crs.com/ (accessed December 20, 2006).

Crawford, Robert J. *The Expert Witness: A Manual for Experts.* Bloomington, IN: AuthorHouse, 2001.

Doyle, Chuck. "Quality and Value—Are They the Same?" Lean Advisors Inc. http://www.leanadvisors.com/ (accessed January 2, 2007).

El Boghdady, Dina. "New Math On the Old Commission." *Washington Post,* November 11, 2006. http://www.washingtonpost.com/ (accessed December 1, 2006).

Higuera, Jonathan J. "Home Builders Feel Ethnic Buyers' Impact." March 8, 2006. http://www.azcentral.com/ (accessed November 15, 2006).

Lee, Michael. *OPENING DOORS: Selling to Multicultural Real Estate Clients.* Winchester, VA: Oakhill Press, 1999.

National Association of REALTORS®. 2005 *National Association of REALTORS® Profile of Home Buyers and Sellers.* http://www.realtor.org/ (accessed December 5, 2006).

National Association of REALTORS®. "The Facts about FSBOs." http://www.realtor.org/research.nsf/pages/fsbofacts (accessed December 5, 2006).

National Association of REALTORS®. "Graduate REALTOR® Institute." http://www.realtor.org/griclear.nsf?OpenDatabase (accessed December 15, 2006).

National Association of REALTORS®. "Home Buyer and Seller Survey Shows Rising Use of Internet, Reliance on Agents." January 17, 2006. http://www.realtor.org/press_room/news_releases/2006/hmbuyersellersurvey06.html (accessed December 5, 2006).

National Association of REALTORS®. "Personal Assistants." http://www.realtor.org/ (accessed December 12, 2006).

Poynter, Dan. *The Expert Witness Handbook: Tips and Techniques for the Litigation Consultant.* Santa Barbara, CA: Para Publishing, 2004.

Pujals, Jerry. *Secrets to Real Estate Success.* Ridgeland, SC: Cameo Publications, 2005, 35.

I n d e x

A

Adriá, Ferrán, 134
Absentee owners, 118
Access, 30, 37
ACT!, 30, 37
Active listening, 48–51
Activities list, 4–6
Advertising, 89–91
Agent Office, 30
Aircard, 31
Aircheck, 208
Amenities, 131
Anger, deflecting, 144–46
Appointments, 173–74
Appraiser relations, 167–68
Articles, 115–17, 208
"Ask the Expert" television program, 208
Assistant, 41, 175–76, 193
Assumptive close, 163
Attire, professional, 151–52
Attitude, 210–11
Awards, 27–28

B

Balanced life, 185–87, 210
Banks, 184
Bargaining, 177–79
Beer brewing party, 120
Beliefs, 74
Ben Franklin close, 163–64
Benefits, 92–95
Bias, 50
Black Belt Negotiating, 178
Blog, 105–7
Board of REALTORS®, 27–30, 56, 98, 208
Body piercing, 153

Brainstorming, 189–90, 202
Brain surgery analogy, 23–24
Brand, 124–26, 207–9
Broker
    charges, 7
    protection clause, 166–67
Bdget, 28
Business plan, 194–96
Business practices
    Buyer-Broker Agreement, 156–58
    career apparel, 154–55
    expenses, 7–8
    name badge, 154–55
    pricing listings, 158–60
    professionalism, 151–54
Buyer
    common problems, 44–46
    disqualification, 44, 45–46
    first-time questions, 42
    guarantee, 166–67
    needs, 3
    questions, 62–63, 93
Buyer-Broker Agreement, 6, 12–13, 66–67, 72, 102, 156–58
Buyers' Guide, 15
Buyers' kit, 71–72

C

Car analogy, 23
Career apparel, 118, 154–55
CC&Rs *See* Covenants, conditions and restrictions
Celebrity, 207–9
Cellular telephone, 30
Certified Financial Planners (CFPs), 182

219